985

Jack Lemmon

Jack Lemmon

Michael Freedland

St. Martin's Press
New York

Illustration Acknowledgments

The photographs in this book are reproduced by kind permission of the following:

Aquarius Picture Library 2 below (© Jonie Taps/Col), 3 above (© Winton Hoch/Leland Hayward), 4 above (© Warwick), 6 (© Fred Kohlmar/Lang), 7 (© Globe), 8 below (© Globe); *BBC Hulton Picture Library* 12 below; *National Film Archive London* 1, 2 above, 3 below, 4 below, 5, 8 above, 9–11, 12 above, 13–16.

The credit for the photograph on the front cover should read *Rex Features*.

JACK LEMMON. Copyright © 1985 by Michael Freeland. All rights reserved. Printed in the United States of America. No part of this book may be used or reproduced in any manner whatsoever without written permission except in the case of brief quotations embodied in critical articles or reviews. For information, address St. Martin's Press, 175 Fifth Avenue, New York, N.Y. 10010.

Library of Congress Cataloging in Publication Data

Freedland, Michael, 1934–
  Jack Lemmon.

  1. Lemmon, Jack.   2. Moving-picture actors and
actresses—United States—Biography.   I. Title.
PN2287.L42F7 1985   791.43'028'0924 [B]   85-2563
ISBN 0-312-43939-3

First published in Great Britain by George Weidenfeld & Nicolson Ltd.
First U.S. Edition
10 9 8 7 6 5 4 3 2 1

To David Freedland
1899–1983

שמע בני פומה אביך

Listen, son, to the teaching of your father. (Proverbs I, 8.)

Contents

Acknowledgments

The first acknowledgment in this book is to its subject, for being perhaps the most outstanding film actor of our age. That, at any rate, is the premise behind writing a biography of Jack Lemmon, twice an Oscar winner, and a performer who has made the trek from light comedy to major dramatic roles, in which one facial gesture can convey the agony of a father searching for the remains of his murdered son.

Jack told me he didn't want a biography written about him at this stage of his career – but, to quote the title of a Lemmon film, I thought he deserved a Tribute. I have twice had the opportunity of interviewing him at length for BBC Radio and for this book I have drawn on these conversations and on interviews with his close friend Walter Matthau. I also spoke to June Allyson, Fred Astaire, Betsy Blair, George Burns, Sammy Cahn, Frank Capra, the late George Cukor, Sandy Dennis, George 'Bullets' Durgan, Steve Forrest, Betty Garrett, Arthur Hiller, Janet Leigh, Charlie Murphy, Bill Orr, Gregory Peck, Veronique Peck, Richard Quine, Walter Scharf, Melville Shavelson and Billy Wilder. To them all my very grateful thanks.

I must also thank Carol Epstein and her colleagues of the library of the Academy of Motion Picture Arts and Sciences, Beverly Hills, and the librarians of the British Film Institute and the British Library.

Above all, to my wife Sara, and our considerate offspring, Fiona, Dani and Jonathan, my gratitude for allowing me to tie myself down to tape recorder and word processor – and my love.

MICHAEL FREEDLAND
London, 1984

Jack Lemmon

I

The Fortune Cookie

Jack Lemmon was born not so much with a silver spoon in his mouth as with a golden doughnut clenched in his fist. By the time he was born his father, John Uhler Lemmon II, had climbed to the vice-presidency of the Doughnut Corporation of America, and was no longer short of the means to provide all that his family could want.

John Lemmon came from an Irish-American background. He had originally hoped to be an entertainer, and following in the footsteps of his uncle, Jimmy O'Toole, who specialized in a 'Dr Jekyll and Mr Hyde' act, he performed in that unique American institution, the minstrel show. He was convinced that he had a successful career ahead of him until one night in San Francisco he was hit by a bottle flung from the audience. He bore the scar for the rest of his life, and he gave up the stage immediately. World War I had in the meantime broken out and at the Annapolis Naval Academy, where his induction was so short that he was known as a 'ninety-day wonder', he was given a commission in the United States Navy. His first voyage was to China, and took up most of his brief war service.

On his return from sea John took a short-term job selling equipment to bakeries, and his Irish charm quickly took him to the position of champion salesman. Despite his success with the company, his restless spirit urged him on to a job which seemed to offer more of a challenge. He joined an advertising agency where he is credited with inventing some of America's best-known campaigns and slogans of the time, including the Planters' peanuts logo – a peanut-shaped man. John Lemmon himself claimed to have invented the Bayer box, the patent aspirin container. His boss was George Washington Hill, the famed advertising king. When advertising finally palled, John moved back into the bakery business, but this time on the product side. Once again a salesman, he travelled extensively in Europe and sold American doughnuts there with an intensity that crusaders for other causes would envy. He is responsible for introducing the doughnut to Britain. It may seem a strange occupation for a man known as a wit, and clearly gifted with both the spoken and written word, and so good-looking as to be relentlessly pursued by a number of women – but not to John Lemmon. 'The day I don't find romance in a loaf of bread,' he later told his son Jack, 'I'll quit.'

In the early 1920s he met Millie La Rue Noel on a blind date. The daughter of a wealthy Baltimore family, she was in her late twenties. John Lemmon, who loved fast cars and was always a snappy dresser who never went out without a bowler or homburg hat, was an immensely attractive and charming partner. They were soon married and settled in a big house in Newton, a suburb of Boston, close to the headquarters of the Doughnut Corporation of America. John continued to travel a great deal in his work, and Millie took up the fashionable and all-absorbing occupation of giving and attending bridge parties and drinking cocktails with the other Boston wives.

They hadn't been married long when Millie discovered a baby was on the way. Unfortunately the child arrived somewhat prematurely, and on 8 February 1925 Millie, who didn't believe it could possibly be happening, and was lingering over a bridge game at the Boston Ladies' Club, had to be rushed to the Newton-Wellesley Hospital with all the speed of an emergency. The baby was born in the hospital lift, on the way to the delivery room. Jack's arrival scared Millie so much that she vowed never to have any more children, and she kept her word, despite her husband's Irish Catholic love of large families.

The boy was given the same names as his father, John Uhler Lemmon III, but he was always to be known as Jack. From the beginning Jack had to get used to people making jokes about his surname. The first was the nurse who saw the slightly jaundiced baby lying in his crib in the hospital and remarked, 'My, what a yellow little lemmon,' and throughout Jack's schooldays he was plagued by cries of 'Hey, Jack, U. Lemmon!'

Jack was allowed to leave the hospital with his mother at the usual time, but he was to have one undescended testicle and had to return to hospital for this and a variety of other operations during his childhood. He had a hernia, mastoids and a permanently blocked nose. He also suffered all the usual childhood illnesses – three times in the operating theatre did not absolve him from coming out in spots with measles or suffering the swollen glands of mumps, followed by both rheumatic fever and scarlet fever. He later said that he had his adenoids out five times and his tonsils out twice. The memory of those endless visits to hospitals and clinics, in the days when surgery of the most painful kind was the only treatment where today benign antibiotics would be prescribed, still makes him shiver. At home he used to try to keep quiet about any physical pain in the hope that he wouldn't have to go into hospital again.

Both his parents were extremely anxious over little Jackie, and never thought that he would grow up to live a perfectly healthy and trouble-free life. He was a pretty baby, but his many illnesses set him back, and he didn't develop physically at the same rate as other children. His father gave him a pony named Pepper in the hope that some outdoor activity would strengthen him, but he only fell off.

He was a late talker, but this could be because in the luxurious Lemmon household he was so cosseted that he had no need to speak – his every wish was taken care of. Then one day during the crisp New England winter a tiny figure muffled in thick clothes was heard to knock on his own front door and to announce, 'I is froze.' He had climbed out of his perambulator and taken matters into his own hands. From then on Jack's formerly underused vocal chords were put to good effect. He started to imitate his mother's friends – and since she was something of a social butterfly, and popular for her great sense of the absurd, there were a number of these – and before long would perform what some said was the best W. C. Fields impersonation Newton had ever

3

seen. Well into adulthood, he would greet friends in true Fields style, 'How are you, m'boy.'

At the same age, the young Lemmon made his début in a play called *Gold in Them Thar Hills*. The star was his father, who was taking time off from selling doughnuts to play in an amateur production for charity. Jack's contribution was a three-word speech, predicting a flood. 'The dam's bust,' were the first words he ever recited in public.

When he was five Jack was sent to the Rivers County Day School, where he showed no great academic ability, but was very popular with his teachers, the way clean-looking boys with neatly cut hair frequently are. He also had a chance to play in one of the school's dramatic productions and was delighted to find that he could make people laugh. It made no difference that what his earliest audiences were laughing at was the fact that at the end of every line he went to the back of the stage to pick up his dialogue from the prompter. To be fair, he was substituting for the 'star' of the show who was away from school with whooping cough.

But he had got hooked on performing, and would entertain people at home with a demonstration of snores. This followed a visit to the cinema with his mother, where a medley of different snores formed the centrepiece of a movie short. When the movie was over, he gave out one of his own, so loud that virtually the whole theatre heard it and responded with a louder burst of applause than at any previous Lemmon dramatic appearance. By the age of seven, he had collected no fewer than twenty-five different examples of this art. His favourite was the freight-train snore. The one he liked least was his father's – which his mother used as the excuse for having separate bedrooms. Even as a small child he saw this move as having special, foreboding significance.

John Lemmon was away from home for weeks at a stretch. In the days before air travel, the journey to Europe and back consumed time that no modern salesman would conceive of giving to a decade's output, let alone a mere season's operations. It left Millie very much on her own, and she and John began to drift apart. When they were together it was only to quarrel. Jack, young though he was, wondered if it had anything to do with him.

He decided that the best thing to do was to stay quiet and behave himself, as though the love he offered his parents in this way would somehow bring them together. He went to mass with his father, while Millie stayed at home or went to the Ritz-Carlton Hotel in Boston where she once threatened to take up permanent residence, although she never ventured much further than the bar. Her attachment to the hotel was such that she twice tried to get the management to agree that they would allow her ashes to be arrayed alongside the bourbon and scotch on the mirrored shelves she had faced so often. She even offered to pay for the privilege. The hotel returned her cheques with thanks, and firm refusals. On church-going Millie would say that she was a Baptist, and Baptists didn't demand the same kind of attendance as Catholics. If she were that much of a Baptist, she would have realized that she belonged to what was essentially a temperance movement, but it was a convenient and seemingly acceptable alternative to going to mass, and Jack accepted it.

Jack would never admit to being troubled by his parents' problems in public, and usually managed to laugh when others would have cried. 'It was his fun and games façade,' said a friend who had been with Jack at his next school, the prestigious Phillips Academy at Andover, Massachusetts. Those who knew him then now claim to have detected misery beneath the antics, as though like a clown he only painted on the fun. 'Jack was a hundred years old when he was fourteen,' his old schoolfriend maintains.

Jack's parents stayed together for their son's sake alone, though they should, he now says, have separated by the time he was ten. Instead they prolonged the agony until his late teens, when Jack was in his last year at Andover. When the break-up finally came, John Lemmon simply moved his clothes out of the house and took a suite at an hotel. The precise reason for the move still escapes Jack, and it certainly perplexed his parents' friends, for the good-looking couple were still fond of each other and never got round to drawing up legal papers concerning their separation. The business of divorce appeared to be too final a step for them to take.

Jack's great solace during these years was his love of music, and particularly the piano. At the age of eleven he had started taking lessons, though his teacher did not note any great aptitude. He would, at that stage, have preferred going out to play baseball, and his neighbours were hardly encouraging. 'The boy next door,' he said later, 'who was two years older than I was, made it very clear that I was a big fat cissy for taking piano lessons.' A year later he was taken to see a movie in which the famous Polish pianist Paderewski played Beethoven's *Moonlight Sonata*. Sitting, not in a concert hall, but in a cinema, he discovered a world that had previously been closed to him – not even a chink of which had been exposed in his home lessons. 'He played this thing and it fractured me. I cried like a baby. It was right afterwards that I started playing by ear ... since then the piano has been one of the main sources of joy in my life. In fact, it's a necessity. If I don't play the piano every couple of days, I get itchy.'

He was a young man of ambition. Smitten by the music of George Gershwin, Jack was determined to be the one who would take on the mantle of the composer of 'The Man I Love', 'S'Wonderful' and 'I Got Rhythm'. Rhythm he definitely had – even though he hadn't learnt (and hasn't to this day) how to put it down on paper or read anyone else's notes.

His other ambition was to become an actor. He was going to be the greatest actor that America ever produced. And if there were the slightest chance of synthesizing those two ambitions by making sweet music while acting on a stage, that was what he wanted above everything else. As for his parents, they were more than happy to encourage the ambition. They knew that, with Lemmon luck, their boy was going to do well.

He didn't shine academically, but there were ways in which he could lead the others – particularly in running. The boy who had been in and out of hospital – and by the time he ceased making this a regular activity, he had chalked up ten operations – was now proving to be the nearest thing to an Andover streak of lightning, since the last thunderstorm. He ran a mile danger-ously close to four minutes at a time when even Roger Ban-nister, a continent away, hadn't thought he would actually break that barrier. He was the sensation of the school's cross-country team, and broke a number of records for boys of his age group.

There was one other achievement he yearned for, but which proved elusive - losing his virginity. He was overcome by awe for the opposite sex. As he told writer Don Widener, when he did finally get to a position where he might manage to kiss a girl he missed her mouth by three inches – but accidentally put his hand on one of the young lady's breasts. Unfortunately, he didn't realize what he had done, and missed the opportunity of discovering at least something about the business of sex.

He seemed to be scoring higher on stage. The school was already aware that he screwed his face into the sort of patterns that not only made people laugh and feel sorry for him at the same time, but which girls thought ridiculously attractive. When they heard him play Gershwin on the school piano, his classmates were convinced that Tin Pan Alley would before long be sending an emissary around to their seat of learning begging him to write either a number to top the hit parade or a score for the next Broadway blockbuster. He wrote a song for the school show – or, rather, like another tunesmith who never learned how to read or write music, Irving Berlin, had someone write it for him. The song was dreadful, but Andover liked it and Jack himself thought that, even if he hadn't yet arrived, he was on his way.

His father, meanwhile, had decided that the place Jack was on his way to was Harvard – the college he himself would love to have attended if only his family could have afforded the fees. Before going there, however, there were the school vacations and the opportunity of the best summer holiday job he could wish for. The Marblehead Players indicated they were willing to take him on as an apprentice in *Burlesque*, the play they were going to put on; it would be starring Bert Lahr, one of America's greatest comedians, whom most poeple knew from his role as the Cowardly Lion in *The Wizard of Oz*.

Jack seems to have had the same effect on the Marblehead management as he had on most of the other people with whom he came into contact: they were enchanted by him. Not least of all Mr Lahr who, not without reason, thought he had found his own personal prodigy in this youth playing a drunk pianist. Jack did everything perfectly – until Lahr discovered he couldn't read music. What did it matter, just so long as he played properly?

Plenty, Lahr decided. What would happen if he forgot what he was supposed to be playing? Well, he might have been told, drunk pianists sometimes *did* forget. It wasn't good enough for Lahr, who by then had had his greatest moments on stage, and Jack had to content himself with a future at Harvard – and a naval uniform.

Jack seemed just right for Harvard in 1943. His clean grey-flannel-suit looks had Ivy League stamped all over them. And if he wasn't right for the football team or played baseball with no enthusiasm, there were compensations. It was a joy to hear him at the piano, especially when he played tunes he had made up himself. The hangers-on were ready to be convined that he really was Gershwin reincarnated. Besides, he made them laugh a lot – with a chuckle of his own like the sound of crushed walnuts.

His academic progress wasn't that good – in fact from the moment he entered the college he was consistently bottom of the class. What worried him, however, was his failure to make any headway with the opposite sex. Today, you would say he was unlucky in bed. Young John Uhler Lemmon III never got that far. He rarely achieved more than a grope in a dark alley, until the day – or rather the night – when at last his virginity became a thing of the past. He didn't enjoy the experience, although by his own account his partner was convinced that he was the greatest lover since Valentino. On this celebrated occasion he found himself a convertible car belonging to someone else, and converted it – into a seduction wagon. It was he who was seduced in the end, but not before he had managed to thrust his leg through the canvas roof of the borrowed vehicle.

But laughs were what he really wanted. One former classmate remembered: 'When we went out to shows, we'd say, "Let's go and see the girls." Jack would say, "No, let's go and see the comics."' And he gave every impression of never wanting to be other than funny himself. He was elected – the first of such honorary offices – runner-up to the Class Clown of 1943. What became of the outright winner of the contest is not on record.

Jack was in naval uniform for much of the time. America was now in World War II and young Lemmon was following in his father's footsteps, joining the naval branch of the college's cadet corps. It was part of a scheme known as the V–12 programme. He didn't enjoy the experience – particularly the early-morning exercises and running he was expected to do. He and his fellow cadets were instructed to run along the banks of the Charles River, but Jack found a way of escaping into the nearby bushes, where he would smoke a cigarette until the rest of the squad came into sight. The corps were usually ordered to do several laps, but Jack would always come out of it all looking bright-eyed and bushy-tailed. One day, however, the instructor was no more keen on the exercise than were his charges. One lap, he said, was enough. That meant that Jack was busy smoking when they were on their way back to base. After forty-five minutes, he was marked AWOL. Not a promising start to a naval career, which fortunately he never planned on having.

The slightest opportunity to escape some of the rigours of this pre-service life was always accepted. One way to get out of early-morning exercises was to play a dawn chorus on the college radio; it was an early audience for the man who knew his own 'Rhapsody in Blue' was just around the corner. His other love was the college dramatic society and he joined the most prestigious show organization in American university life, the Hasty Pudding Club. In 1945 he was ready to run for presidency in the club against a fellow student named Appel. By two votes, the members decided they preferred a Lemmon pudding to an Appel one. He wrote the 1945 club show, *The Proof of the Pudding* – including the piano interlude – and most people who came to see it left feeling that the name of one of the sacred traditions of Harvard had not been taken in vain. His song for this show was 'The Bottom's Fallen Out of Everything But You'. In a more serious vein, playing an old man, he was the star attraction in the college version of *The Playboy of the Western World* by J. M. Synge. No one who saw it is on record as suggesting that they foresaw Lemmon's dramatic performances as the star of such films as *Days of Wine and Roses* and *Save the Tiger*. But it was impressive – especially to the woman in the audience who was buffeted in the face by the two black wax false teeth that Jack accidentally spat out in his first oration.

There was nothing to dislike in Jack Lemmon and a great deal to admire. He had all the insecurities of youth, and a persistent

9

anxiety about his parents, but as most of the people with whom he came into contact would testify, he didn't show many of these fears. At the Dramatic Club and the Delphic Club he was Harvard's blue-eyed boy who never threw his weight around; he had no need to do so. He was Vice-President of both organizations while still holding the Hasty Pudding headship. It was the stuff college dreams were made of.

He earned some spare cash – always a college boy's prime requisite, although Mr Lemmon Senior made sure there was never a wolf even close to his door – playing at a local bar. Jack says that he played by request. Half the people requested tunes they wanted to hear; the other half asked him to stop playing.

His dedication to piano-playing impressed his father, which Jack might have considered reward enough. He said later, 'I had a combination of love and respect and awe for my father. And there is no question that I did want to impress him.' It was the kind of need that a boy feels when he first gets close to a girl. He knows he wants to be with her, but can't feel really sure that she feels the same way. Jack was never totally relaxed in his father's presence. 'It wasn't that he put demands on me. This was just purely me wanting to measure up.' To many people, John Lemmon was the personification of the American Dream, like a Huckleberry Finn who had become President of General Motors. Although he felt almost the same way about his professors and the other instructors at Harvard this feeling never had the same urgency as his need to scale up to what he – sometimes erroneously – believed were his father's demands and definitions of perfection.

Jack's scholastic achievements were aided in no small way by one of the factors that made his dramatic début so promising – a photographic memory. He managed to remember enough just to scrape through his examinations, even though much of his time was spent on what Harvard delicately called 'probation'. One of the requirements of probation was that he concentrate on his studies to the exclusion of all other activities – which included his theatrical exploits – so he decided it was safer to operate under a pseudonym. Now what *nom de théâtre* could Jack Lemmon choose? Timothy Orange seemed to cover his needs.

Certainly, the teaching staff at Harvard were less than excited by the academic potential young Lemmon seemed to present. The Dean told him: 'Lemmon, you'll never amount to a thing.' His Latin professor was only slightly less scathing: 'You've got brains, Lemmon,' he said. 'But they're scattered. Collect 'em.'

Jack might have been more concerned about such statements had he not been sure, with all the certainty of youth, that he was going to be either a top actor or a master composer. By this time he had settled for a future in acting, with a little music on the side – because he seemed to have had more luck in that direction. If he were going to starve in an off-off-off-Broadway garret, nothing that had happened so far seemed to give any indication of that possibility. Years later, he saw the folly of such optimism: 'I still wake up in a cold sweat sometimes and ask myself, Jesus, what would you have done if you hadn't become an actor? I just don't know.'

But in 1945 the United States Navy decided that his fate was working for them. Almost reluctantly, they commissioned him as an ensign, an ensign whose career accorded almost exactly with a certain Mr Pulver who would destroy the historically held values of the US Navy in the movie *Mister Roberts*.

Now, the first thing anyone gets to know about Jack Lemmon is that he possesses an inherent modesty which protests that everything in which he succeeds is the result of some dreadful accident and miraculous coincidence. The notion hardly does him justice, but the truth sometimes sounds awfully like the centre pages of a Jack Lemmon film script. When he took his naval entrance exam in physics, he answered the first two questions perfectly – and then couldn't solve a single one of the other problems. The trauma this presented had a profound effect. He was violently sick. His examiners took one look at the first two perfectly answered questions and decided that he probably would have answered the others correctly – had he not been struck so ill. He was not so lucky with the other subjects. He was told in no uncertain terms that his average was the lowest anyone could ever remember being allowed to qualify for the wardroom – anywhere. But America *was* at war, so almost anything could be justified. And both Germany and Japan were sufficiently on the run for Jack Lemmon not to be considered any great liability either. No one at the time knew, however, that he had more interest in being a new John Barrymore than in winning any battles.

He was totally out of place in the Navy. As he later said: 'I was so bloody consumed with myself that I wasn't aware of what was going on around me. I had no social conscience whatsoever. I don't even think I was aware the war was on. Honest to God, and I was in the Navy.' He had no natural feeling for either the traditions of the service or for the salt spray of the sea. But he came from Harvard and it was from there that the senior officers of the aircraft carrier USS *Lake Champlain* were expecting a communications officer to come.

Now Jack knew that when he sat down to his piano he was communicating. He had finally managed to communicate his natural urges to a number of pretty girls, and when he stood on a stage he was at the beginning of a demonstration in communication with his fellow players that would before long become legendary. But communications in a ship? 'I didn't know a flag from a blinker,' he admitted.

The huge ship was lying at anchor at Norfolk, Virginia and as far as he could see was in the process of being totally dismembered. All the guns were being stripped. Masses of other equipment were being taken ashore and as far as Ensign Lemmon was concerned the only thing he had to do was to accomplish much the same task for the communications machinery – everything from telegraphic instruments to the flags. No one told him that this floating airbase had to proceed to Newport News, another harbour in Virginia – and when the *Lake Champlain* drew away from her anchorage it was without a single piece of equipment that would inform any other vessel that she was on her way.

And where, in particular, was the vital flag that had to be flown when a ship leaves port? This was the start of the Lemmon coincidence story, the first of his seaborne nine lives. One flag had *not* been taken ashore. Just one. The single flag that hadn't been spotted by Ensign Lemmon was *the* flag, the one they needed. Later, the ship almost collided with a tanker. Jack told the captain that it looked as if the smaller vessel had a screw loose. It did –

there was something wrong with one of its propellers – and the captain, who as a result of Jack's diagnosis steered his giant clear of trouble, awarded the youngest officer on board top performance marks.

After that, he got a posting more suitable to his talents – in charge of a Navy car pool. He was delighted. Only seven months after he had first saluted the flag as a commissioned officer, the US dropped its atom bombs on Hiroshima and Nagasaki. The war ended at about the same time as the career of Ensign John Uhler Lemmon III. The Navy had convinced him of one thing beyond all doubt: as a sailor, he was a damned good actor. Now his ambition was to show to someone, somewhere, that as an actor he was also a pretty good actor.

His next step was to go back to Harvard to graduate. He didn't have any great hopes of coming away with honours, but if nothing else his exemplary war service would almost guarantee that he would be awarded his degree.

But first there was the summer before that last college session to fill in. There was only one thing for him to do – work in a stock company. The North Shore Players in his own state of Massachusetts seemed to offer most possibilities. The company had an enviable reputation – both for the work that it did and for the people in it – and he wanted to join it. He had to audition for the part of Miller in *Young Woodley*, a famous play about a British public school. The title role was taken by Roddy McDowall, whose mother was manager of the company. Mrs McDowall was showing her usual concern for detail and one by one she turned down the applicants for Miller because they didn't sound English enough – even though a few boys really were from England. Eventually it was Jack's turn. He took a deep breath and went into the boy's lines sounding as English as he could. It is a harder test of an American actor's skills than may at first be imagined. Halfway through, the raucous sound of Mrs McDowall's voice interrupted him from the stalls. 'Thank God for an English voice,' she called. The part was his. He developed the accent and took the part of a Cockney in another play, *Adam the Creator*, which the company put on briefly during the summer. Although an early appearance with the North Shore Players, in a tiny part in *Angel*

Street, was marred by his neglecting to try on his hat and having it collapse over his eyes on the first night, he managed to convince both Mrs McDowall and the summer audience that he was worth having, and his acting was well received.

In the autumn he returned to Harvard for the final year before his degree, which he managed to get – just – in the subject of war material management. But his studies didn't interest him then any more than they had before. All he wanted to do was to go to New York, and once there, Broadway. He was going to take the American stage by storm, and he was going to take over where George Gershwin left off. There were to be no half measures.

2
The Entertainer

'Boy, when I started out in acting, what wasn't I going to do!' Jack said later of his Broadway pipe-dream. 'Going by train from my home in Boston to New York I was too excited to sit down. There I was on my way to do two great things – save Broadway and put American music back on its feet, which it hadn't been since the death of Gershwin. Unfortunately they wouldn't let me do either of those things.'

While he saw that getting to the top might take a little time he simply didn't recognize that getting a job at the bottom of the theatre tree, or even at the roots, was harder than doing without food. And if he didn't achieve the former the latter was more than likely.

He made the trek with his father's blessing and limited financial backing to the tune of $300, which even in 1946 was no fortune. Jack didn't want to be dependent on his father, and his father probably had a sneaking notion that this was the sensible way of ensuring that his son would really get to grips with what he was planning. It was sufficient to stake his early weeks in New York, make sure that he would find a bed to sleep in and a hamburger to eat, but not enough to guarantee Jack a life of subsidized idleness. John Lemmon would have been happier to welcome his son into the bakery business, but all the same he gave him some of the benefit of his own working experience. It was all a question of salesmanship – not of product. 'No,' he said, 'you have to sell yourself.' Jack never forgot that conversation.

'Dad would have loved me to enter his business, but all he said was, "You love acting? You need it? You must do it."'

Jack did it – in the way a thousand other actors had done before and have done since. He lodged in a fleapit hotel close enough to Broadway both to smell the greasepaint and to hear the crowds, and haunted the agents' offices. For the first time the Lemmon confidence was dented. The pride of Harvard who had scraped through his exams but scored in every popularity contest, the naval officer who had bluffed admirals, was now neither enchanting nor even communicating. He was – and that could have been great experience, if it wasn't so downright depressing – suffering in a way he hadn't done since he was dragged off to hospital for those ten operations.

Whenever he could, he found a piano to while away the hours. Occasionally he bumped into friends, but he tried to keep them at bay for much the same reason that he didn't write or ring home to Boston very often – he wasn't exactly proud that he hadn't found any work.

It wasn't long before he took the opportunity of leaving the cramped hotel to join a friend in a small apartment on Delancey Street, the heart of the area immortalized in the first talkie, Al Jolson's *The Jazz Singer*, nineteen years earlier. Jack was persuaded that sharing the rent made economic sense and that the new set-up would be great for entertaining the comely young women whom he could enchant with his piano, playing at the parties to which he managed to get himself invited. Not all the girls appreciated the folklore atmosphere of Delancey Street – or some of the smells emanating from the Isaac Gellis delicatessen down below, reputed to be the oldest in America. Also, Jack had to work hard at his patter when it came to fulfilling the promises he had made. Getting a girl into bed could be hard enough – as his friend in the room next door was frequently discovering. Jack had to get them into the bath, because that was where he was sleeping.

Living over the delicatessen did have its advantages: occasionally the landlord let him have some of his kosher sausages. And the location did provide some marvellous acting experience, although that was not the way it was planned. One morning, Jack left his bedroom for his first visit of the day to the only lavatory in the building. He didn't bother to take his usual precaution of leaving the door on the latch. After going only a few steps, he heard it close. There was no one in the building who had a key, and he was in his vest and pants. The landlord had one, but he was in the shop, and the only way to reach that was through the street. It was February and very cold and snowy, as it can so easily be in New York in February. The only thing to do was to pretend that it was the most natural occurrence in the world. He walked on to the pavement, his head in the air, certain that if he didn't see anyone, no one would see him. He marched into the delicatessen, addressed the landlady who was deep in conversation with a customer about the price of pickled cucumbers and said: 'Good morning. This is Lemmon of apartment 5A. I seem to have locked myself out. Could I have the key, please?' Without looking up from her cucumbers, the woman gave Jack the key and he walked out of the shop, on to the street and back through the hallway of the apartment building – certain to this day that no one noticed him, let alone what he was wearing.

Another friend let him use his apartment and his piano. He also had a very distinguished fur-trimmed coat which Jack took to borrowing. Once he wore it on his daily trip round the agents' offices, and as a result found himself an agent. The man wasn't able to find him any work, but he did offer to buy the coat – repeatedly.

He occasionally managed to earn a dollar or two thanks to his subsidiary occupation of piano-player to the drinking masses, and when he did write home his letters owed more to imagination than truth. When the *Saturday Evening Post* asked him once about how tough it all was, he replied: 'Tough is a flabby word for it, friend.'

He took a room in one place that cost him the grand sum of a dollar and a half a week – half as much as his first hotel had charged per night. He described it as a ' . . . darling room. I could watch the world through my transom.' It had walls decorated in puce. But there was a piano and that was all that seemed to count. For hour after hour he could slouch over the keys in the pose that others would come to recognize as unique. There are concert pianists who sit down on a stool, the glistening white keys before them like a row of pearly teeth, and look like ramrods. Lemmon looked then, and he looks now, like a rag doll at the end of a hard night.

Persistence was, however, to pay off – not much in financial terms, but a decided improvement on the way things had been going up till then. He got a job working at a Second Avenue dive much admired by aspiring young showpeople such as himself who regarded the early starving years – or at least told themselves that they did – as an essential part of the apprenticeship for their calling.

The place was the Old Knick, run by Paul Killiam, who had first seen Jack at Harvard. Although it was totally different in concept, the name obviously owed something to London's Old Vic, at one time the Royal Victoria Hall – the Old Knick was formerly the Old Knickerbocker Music Hall. The waiters received no salary but lived on tips from customers who came to enjoy the acts they put on between trips to and from the kitchen. Among them were Cliff Robertson, Jack Albertson and Maureen Stapleton. Lemmon was both waiter and master of ceremonies. When the tips weren't that big, he lived on tomato soup.

He couldn't afford new clothes, a staple requirement for an actor who should always look as though he doesn't need the job he is desperate to get. It all required the one asset he did have in plenty – confidence. People told him that only one person in a thousand would really make it in show business. Well, he was going to be *that* one – even if all the available evidence was to the contrary.

Seven of the players at the Old Knick decided that there were better ways of investing the $14 which between them they were spending in rent – and that was by occupying a disused building they had discovered near West 40th Street. They could invest the saved $14 on props for their show. They bought sleeping bags and settled down. For the first night everything went according to plan. The second night was perfect, too. By the time the third and fourth nights came, they reckoned they were hardy troupers who between them had beaten the problems of New York's intense housing shortage.

It was at eight o'clock on the fourth morning that they awoke to see a shape careering close to them – the shadow of a huge crane. With a huge steel ball on its end. The ball crashed through a window, bricks flew everywhere and the ceiling collapsed. Within two minutes, the seven troupers were out of the shell – just in time to see the whole building collapse. Inside were their shoes, socks and most of their clothing. The $14 went on instant replacements for all that stood between them and arrest for a combination of indecency and vagrancy.

Things were to look up before it was too late. Jack's father moved the head office of his doughnut operation to New York and rented a suitable apartment for a man of his calibre. Then he went to see where Jack was living. Years later, when such privations were only memories, Jack said: 'When I opened the door, and he saw the inside of that apartment, his mouth just fell open. I had not been what you might consider an outstanding student and I think he felt he'd gotten me through all those schools by the skin of his teeth, and when he'd finished looking around and gotten his jaw together again, all he could say hoarsely was "Harvard".'

So for a time Jack moved in with his father – and accepted the occasional subsidy to his practically non-existent income. But his comfortable living quarters didn't persuade Jack to change his lifestyle. At the Old Knick, he would start a new show every time a new paying customer entered the bar. Sometimes there were fifteen performances in an evening. When things looked as though they were slackening off, he would play the master of ceremonies to the audience as well as to his fellow artists.

'I'll bet any of you,' he would say, 'I can sing "By the Sea" faster than you can.' His offer was always the same, a bottle of champagne.

'A good thing I always won,' he said. 'There wasn't a bottle of champagne in the joint.' His customers were strictly of the beer and spirits variety. Providing he didn't ever have to fork out for that bubbly, he was less worried now about financial stability. He had discovered, in his second year of struggling, that he could live more or less comfortably on $5 a week.

For a time he gave new life to his notion of becoming the second George Gershwin. One of his friends got him an appointment with a music publisher. Jack played one of his own compositions – and promptly forgot the lyrics. That was the moment he finally decided to stick to the stage.

Even so, he kept on composing, sometimes on the mouth organ. These are some of the titles he wrote, though not all of them were recorded: 'Won't You Be My Chorus for Tonight', 'The Bar-Stool Blues', 'Belly Roll Concerto for French Horn and Ukulele' and 'Row Out the Bathtub and I'll Do a Bubble Dance for You'. To say nothing of 'Lucy Isn't Goosey Any More'.

Then came what must now be regarded as his first foothold off-Broadway, though it was so far it was practically off the map. But it was an acting job. The Ethnological Dance Hall, which didn't sound like a theatre any more than it really sounded like a dance hall, was presenting a version of Tolstoy's *Power of Darkness*, and Jack was offered a part.

It was so hot there, he said, that 'most of the audience fainted'. Not only was it in the middle of a summer heatwave but workmen were manning pneumatic drills outside, day and night, and it was impossible to open a window. Jack stood on stage in a temperature approaching 115°F while people keeled over one by one. There were times when he found it difficult not to copy the audience's example – but he didn't have another seat or a neighbour's lap to fall into. It was the humour of this that kept him upright. Another reason he didn't want to make a fool of himself was that he was basking in the admiration for his acting expressed by another member of the company, a pretty fair-haired girl from Peoria, Illinois, called Cynthia Stone. Jack, Cynthia said, 'thought he was going to be one of the great dramatic actors of all time', and she agreed with him. And Jack, who had previously regarded all girls only as partners for whatever conveniently served as a bed, fell totally, completely and madly in love with her. They had a brief separation when Jack did a short tour with another summer stock company, the Hayloft Theatre at Allentown, Pennsylvania, but when he returned to New York they both knew they were going to get married.

That being so, they had to set about earning a living for themselves. Always in the hope that the big parts would soon come their way, Cynthia managed to find jobs for both of them.

They were to be a pair of poor men's Egon Ronays, checking the food and service in Childs' chain of restaurants. Not only would they eat free, they would get paid as well. Jack had to order meals and then write reports on them. But the idea of Jack writing a poor report about anyone – let alone a waiter who would be likely to suffer from it – is inconceivable. His boss expected constructive comments on whether or not the man poured soup down a lady's back, or coughed over a salad, but Jack gave every single waiter a number-one rating.

It may justifiably be presumed that Jack had other ideas than remaining a food critic for the rest of his life, and that he stoically accepted being fired as just another blow on his way to success. It may also come as no surprise that when he was given a 'yes' at an audition, he didn't treat it as some kind of divine right.

He went to auditions because it was the only way of landing a job. With only eight per cent of New York actors earning their living in their chosen profession, attending them always had an air of wishful thinking about it. The auditions were the talk of all the young out-of-work players at places like the Old Knick. They read about them in *Variety*, gossiped about them in their tenement hideouts over less than clean mugs of instant coffee or – in Jack's case – bowls of tomato soup.

When he heard the NBC were planning to cast a new character for their soap opera *The Brighter Day* he was almost the last of fifteen or so hopefuls to go to the audition. Radio was a closed book to him and when he was given a script to read, he either paced around the floor out of microphone range or practically tore the controls out of the production booth by shouting too loudly.

The producer, Art Hanna, was kind enough to suggest that it might be a good idea if he read the script again – and tried a couple of different interpretations of the role of Bruce. Since Jack knew he didn't have the slightest chance of landing the part, he gave the interpretations a considerable amount of variation. When it was all over, Mr Hanna asked if he had a telephone-answering service – it was the days before answering machines. He said yes – after all he said he spoke to Cynthia every day and she was sure to be able to take any messages that needed passing on. Then he asked why.

Hanna's secretary said simply, 'You've got the job.'

He was so overwhelmed that he snatched up his hat, coat and briefcase and ran all the way to Cynthia's apartment to tell her the good news.

When he went to see her again later that evening he accused her of having a strange man in the flat. He pointed in the direction of that hat, coat and briefcase. 'They're yours,' she said. 'Mine?' He looked inside the briefcase. It had 'Art Hanna' penned on the lid.

Jack apologized profusely to his producer and didn't lose the job. The part of Bruce wasn't exactly Hamlet, but it gave him a year's steady employment, at $75 for three shows a week, and an income the size of which he now wondered how he had ever done without.

If he didn't like the part he was given, he decided to find a way of what he told me he called 'working in counterpoint, frustrating the character as the author had written it'. He said, 'I'd recite the lines the way they had been written but pretend I was talking through a bathroom door. Or that the girl I was talking to had bad breath.' It was a means of putting life into a script that Jack reckoned had none of its own. 'I never did it for a good script, though,' he emphasized.

Another soap opera called *The Road of Life* wanted an actor to play the brother of the main character, a doctor. Jack landed the job and an increase in salary which was roughly double his original fee. On one occasion, on a live broadcast, he read the doctor's lines as well as his own, sending the main character out of the studio in disgust and the producer rolling on the floor in virtual apoplexy as Jack answered his own questions and stumbled through the show. He fluffed more on radio with a typed script in front of him than he ever was to do on stage or television, where he was always able to hide behind the facial expressions he shows his audiences.

It was still the golden age of radio. The habit of being glued to a radio set which stayed on from early in the morning until bedtime had grown steadily during the late 1930s and become a way of life during the war years. It was not an easy practice to break, and there seemed no reason to do so. People were, however, beginning to discover something new – the tiny screens that were slowly becoming status symbols. Few people at the time had television sets, but those that did had them on whenever anything, literally anything, was being shown, and were consequently deserting their radios.

Young actors were beginning to grasp that the daily TV play, always live because no one had yet found a way of recording the black-and-white telecasts, presented them with a totally new market. One of the best of these was the Kraft Theatre. Kraft, the cheese manufacturers, were huge sponsors of shows and their *Kraft Music Hall*, starring Al Jolson, was just about the biggest thing at the time. There were still reputable actors who didn't consider television to be wholly decent, a factor that presented opportunities to youngsters like Jack who thought any chance of showing themselves well worth taking. Kraft were putting on *The Arrival of Kitty*, a skit on *Charley's Aunt*. Jack was given the title role.

The play was followed by others, in several of which he continued to demonstrate his need to operate in 'counterpoint'. In one, he pretended throughout the whole action – again live – to be left-handed. Everything he did through the play was with his left hand. Nobody remarked on it – and that pleased him. 'I wanted it to seem natural,' he told me. 'Not even the director spotted it, I was glad to see.' It was much more difficult to play a well-written part, 'because interesting people don't behave in a predictable manner. We may behave in one way. We may behave in another. So selection is what drives you crazy. Something has to be there to make me itch – and go through that delicious hell of trying to find a character.'

It was after this first television work that he found his way to Worthington Minor, producer of an Irish play, *Shadow and Substance*, which was about to be put on by CBS. By this time Jack realized that you didn't write polite letters to producers and hope you will be called for a discussion before the play is cast.

He invited himself along to Mr Minor's room and told him he was Irish – he had been practising a James Cagney accent all day, the nearest to the real thing that he could get. 'I'm from the Abbey Players in Dublin, yer know,' he said and the producer appeared to accept it in good faith. Minor said he also had relatives in Ireland

and wouldn't it be touching the Blarney Stone if they knew Mr Lemmon's family as well. Then he asked for full details of life at the Abbey, Ireland's most prestigious dramatic company.

Before Jack could manufacture some convincing answers, Minor stepped in. 'I saw you on the Kraft show last Wednesday, you phoney,' he said. 'And you're about as Irish as Eddie Cantor.'

All the same, Minor gave him the role. In fact, he was well aware that there were distinct advantages in that deception. Jack Lemmon might be a phoney, but Minor could have been convinced – even if Eddie Cantor was never very Irish. Also in the play was another unknown who was to do fairly well for himself, Charlton Heston. Both made about $50, but they were working. More important, they were working well enough to be noticed.

It was the beginning of Lemmon's screen career, even if the screen was rarely bigger than fifteen inches across and always in black-and-white – and more often than not you saw a piece of scenery waving about or the shadow of a boom mike. In two years he did about five hundred shows, graduating from walk-on parts to leads in the Robert Montgomery series, as well as other work in the Kraft Theatre. In 1949 he appeared in a series on ABC-TV called *That Wonderful Guy*. Cynthia was in it, too.

The following year he was host on *Toni Twin Time*, in which he deputized for Arthur Godfrey, then as big a name on American television as Alka Seltzer. As usual, Jack was modest when he remembered that show. 'I was the world's worst. We had some good people like Carl Reiner, but somehow the show was terrible and I was out of work for nine months after doing it.'

But without anyone knowing it, Jack made his big-screen début in early 1950. No one knew because there was no billing for him or for any of the other actors. He played a GI in *Once Too Often*, a film made by the United States Army Signal Corps. It was perfect casting. Jack's GI was a klutz who found trouble when no one else would have known it existed.

Jack was already becoming known as a comedian – which was great when he was making people laugh on television but which he found somewhat limiting when it came to applying for other parts which he wanted. He was still at the stage when he accepted not quite all but most of the parts he was offered. What distinguished him from other actors was that he was very good in practically everything he touched. Even though Jack wasn't often out of work, he pretended to be. He haunted his old dives, put on soiled clothes. 'I didn't want to be different from my friends,' he told me.

Some of his friends got married. Jack wasn't different on this count either. He and Cynthia decided that the time had come when they too had to regularize their relationship.

Their wedding was fixed for 7 May 1950 at Peoria. Cynthia's parents made all the arrangements. The Lemmon parents were both coming, although separately. When the day came, however, only the Stone family and John Lemmon were there. Millie didn't turn up. Before the ceremony got under way, Jack found out why.

Mrs Lemmon had been with friends at the bar of the Ritz-Carlton. She had been drinking at the same time as taking a whole variety of pills prescribed by her doctor, who was concerned about her general poor health and the fact that she was sleeping badly. She was in a daze when she came home and put on her gas stove to cook a meal for herself. Only she forgot to light the stove. Neighbours smelt gas, broke into her apartment and took her off to hospital while her only child was standing at the altar with his new bride.

There was no doubt that the gassing was an accident, but it was a time for serious thought nevertheless. Jack got on well with his mother and appreciated her bizarre sense of humour; now he had to worry over her as well.

When he did find work again, it was another television series. In this one he and Cynthia joined three or four other players in what, none too brightly, was called *The Ad-Libbers*. They worked with no scripts. All the sketches they were called on to do were performed ad lib, like a charade, which was exactly what the show was. It flopped miserably. But more and more people were watching Jack, and if 1951 wasn't a vintage year, it was one when people in the business started taking mental and then actual note of his name. Of those days Jack later said, 'There was tremendous excitement in television. There wasn't much money. Everybody was learning and they were willing to experiment. Now there's a lot of dough involved and no one wants to try anything, or anybody, new.'

He and Cynthia were then hired for *The Couple Next Door* on ABC in which they did quarter-hour segments in a show starring Don Ameche and Frances Langford. They were playing newly-weds just like themselves, and most welcome to them was the fee – $1,000 a week for a five-day week. The show itself had plenty to commend it. 'God, that was the best,' Jack said. 'Nobody was important and nobody had anything to lose. Which is a very, very important thing. We had just one fifteen-minute rehearsal.'

On one occasion, a cameraman noticed that Jack's fly was open. 'This cameraman kept following me, close up, wherever I went, so you could see only my head. I thought this guy was crazy. God, I miss it!' Both Jack and Cynthia – Cynnie, as he called her – thought so. Neither of them had ever been better off.

Jack then did a series called *Heaven for Betsy*. CBS put out the fifteen-minute plays, alternating them with Perry Como shows. This venture lasted for a not altogether happy seven months, so when in April 1953 an opportunity came for a part on Broadway Jack jumped at it. He was offered a lead role in a revival of the 1937 play *Room Service* at the Playhouse Theatre. This was the story of a play's producer (John Randolph) and cast being locked up in a hotel while they hope an 'angel' will be found to back their production. Jack played the writer and Everett Sloane, veteran of the film *Citizen Kane* and other work with Orson Welles, was the director.

The *New York Times* quite liked it, and in Jack's first notice in the paper its critic wrote: 'Bartlett Robinson's hotel manager, Jack Lemmon's playwright and Stanley Pragers as the producer's aide-de-camp are all fine.' Unfortunately, the customers weren't so sure. The play, unlike most productions for which the butchers of Broadway put away their sharp knives, was a flop.

For Jack himself, however, it was rather luckier. As always, the people who did buy tickets for the play were the scouts. Some remembered him from television, but not many. TV was still something that serious show business or theatrical types tried not to have to see. All the same they wrote the name Jack Lemmon in their notebooks.

They weren't all lucky. Some put ideas to Jack that he wasn't interested in; others tried to interest managements in a play for which Jack wasn't right. Bill Orr, head of the television division of Warner Brothers, reported back to the studio boss, Jack L. Warner – who was also his father-in-law – on this young actor whom he had already spotted on the small screen. 'When I saw him on Broadway, I knew that he had something very special to offer us. But Warner wasn't interested,' Bill told me. 'We were doing a sort of *Hollywood Canteen* type of film for the troops in Korea and I thought Jack would be just right for that. I thought he had a glowing personality.' But Warner said there was no point in spending a lot of money on an unknown actor for whom nobody was going to pay good cash at the box office.

And Lemmon himself didn't have a great deal of respect for what Warner Brothers was turning out in Hollywood at the time. As he admitted to the *Saturday Evening Post*: 'I hadn't cared much about movies until then. I was strictly a drugstore actor, one of those ambitious kids who sit at a counter, stretch a coffee, and tell each other how great they are. Part of the deal was that every once in a while you had to say, "The hell with the movies." Nobody is more dedicated to Broadway than an actor who has never had a Hollywood offer. In my own mind I was a young guy who'd come down from Boston to save the theatre – only nobody would let me save it.'

But Harry Cohn, the iron dictator of Columbia Pictures, whose principal aim in life seemed to be to spite his opposition, thought otherwise. Max Arnow, one of the legendary names in the history of the Hollywood studios and Columbia's talent manager, saw *Room Service* and almost immediately afterwards recognized the actor in a live television play. He told Cohn he could be the fellow he was looking for to play Judy Holliday's boyfriend in what subsequently became *It Should Happen to You*. At that time, it was *We've Never Been Licked*, which wasn't quite Jack Lemmon's motto but could have been.

As he said, he hadn't been able either to save Broadway or put American music back on its feet, so he agreed to settle for

Hollywood. Just so long as no one thought he was there permanently and wouldn't do the other things some day – and before very long, too. Such confidence signals the difference between journeymen performers and real stars.

He was not free of trouble at the time, however. Jack's relationship with Cynthia was such that few knew of the growing strains that existed. Every effort that he made was geared towards his career. It was a familiar story in show business – the dedicated performer who thinks he is earning money to keep his family living comfortably, while in fact it is only serving to break up the relationship. Later Jack would regret it, but for the moment there was only one way he was going – to the top. While he was working on Broadway, Cynthia told him she was leaving the fashionable apartment they had taken on Sutton Place and was going back to her parents.

Jack, meanwhile, *had* to think about Hollywood. With slightly less enthusiasm than might have been expected he agreed to a screen test. It was directed by Richard Quine who before long would become one of his closest friends.

Quine remembers the moment very well. He told me: 'Max Arnow called me into his office and said, "I want you to do me a favour and do a test of a young kid I've just brought out from New York," and it turned out to be Jack Lemmon. I was marvellously impressed. It was a test that had to be sent off to Harry Cohn and would either make or break Jack at Columbia.'

Jack did two tests with Quine. The first was for *We've Never Been Licked*, and the second for *The Long Gray Line*, a film being made about West Point in which Jack would have to go from a young cadet to an old man. It was as much a challenge for the make-up department as it was for Jack himself. Not only did they have to add lines and folds to his baby face with the aid of clay but they had to pad out his neck and girth. 'The first part of the test was with a lovely actress called Elizabeth Frazer and he was brilliant. Absolutely brilliant,' said Quine. 'Then we waited for him to change into his eighty-year-old's make-up.' That was a different situation. 'He looked so ridiculous that I just couldn't look at him. I couldn't say "Action". I mumbled "Action" and turned my head away. It just didn't make sense.' The baby-faced

Lemmon looked, he said, ludicrous. 'I'd give anything to get my hands on that film today. It has to be a classic, it was so funny. Lemmon was hysterical.'

No one was that enthusiastic about *The Long Gray Line* test, although it showed an actor who was extraordinarily able in the young man part. The earlier test, however, looked better every time Quine and other Columbia executives saw it.

As Quine predicted, Jack was selected to play in *It Should Happen to You*, the story of a model who rents a vast New York poster site, just so that she can see her name pasted up in public view. This was exactly the fate awaiting Jack Lemmon – only others would be spending the money to do it.

3
The Front Page

Hollywood was going to make him. Jack the optimist was sure of that. What no one could have imagined was how quickly it was going to make him and for how long it was all going to last. Said Richard Quine, 'I must confess I didn't think he would be that good – so good that Jack had to tell me to put more into my directing. I told him I liked the way he did it anyway.'

As it was, when he first arrived at the Columbia Studios buildings on Vine Street Cohn and his yesmen – for the studio boss ruled his empire with a rod of red-hot celluloid – paced the room and couldn't decide what to do with their new find. That wasn't unusual. Moguls had had similar problems with Clark Gable and Errol Flynn, and even if Jack Lemmon did have more acting talent than those two combined, it couldn't be assumed that he would more easily make a fortune for his studio.

They certainly didn't think he was worth investing too much on for openers. Instead of putting him up at either the Beverly Wilshire or the Beverly Hills Hotel, they installed him in a room at the downtown Roosevelt Hotel. The first move Jack made was a sensible one on his part. He rang the William Morris Agency, who were representing him. They obviously felt the need to show their client respect more than his new employers did, and they suggested meeting for a drink at the highly prestigious Polo Lounge at the Beverly Hills. Now the Polo Lounge is where important Hollywood deals are done. It is also where couples not necessarily married to each other manage to meet for quiet tête-à-têtes. For while anybody who is anybody goes there, it is so dark in the room you can't always be sure who you actually see.

On this occasion, the conversation at Jack's table was equally opaque. All the talk of percentages and residuals was baffling to a young man who thought he was about to become a film star and now saw he was merely a piece of business machinery. During the meeting Jack went to the men's room and returned through the gloom, sat down at the table and smiled at the flannel-suited men next to him. By now the conversation was even less easy to follow. It took him twenty minutes to realize why the discussion was so mystifying. He had sat down at the wrong table – he was in a business meeting of the rival CMA Agency. His own agents hadn't missed him at all, and none of the CMA men seemed to bother that he was with them.

When he finally got on to the studio floor and began work on the film, the director George Cukor was not sparing in his demands. Jack thought he was doing splendidly, but every time he began a speech Cukor came over to him with firm instructions about not going over the top.

'Don't you want me to act at all?' the new star asked the veteran director.

'Ah, dear boy,' said Cukor. 'You're finally getting it.'

Cukor was, however, exceedingly impressed. 'I don't think I've ever known a more natural actor, a more brilliant comedy performer,' he told me shortly before his death. 'But I remember knowing right at that moment that there would be a time when he would be just as good as a more serious dramatic actor. There was something deep down that made me realize that. His work was so true.' Cukor was a man with a reputation for directing women with a touch that resembled dusting by a sheet of gossamer. He was one of Katharine Hepburn's closest friends. His reputation with men wasn't nearly as firm, yet with Jack Lemmon he had a triumph.

Jack didn't realize it at first. He acted cautiously. But he had several things going for him. One of them was that Cynthia wanted to return to him and would soon join him in Hollywood. He took a cheapish apartment and bought a second-hand car – which cost him so much in repairs that he decided before long, like many another economy-minded motorist, that it would be cheaper to buy a brand-new one.

One night, with Cynthia still back East, he invited Judy Holliday out for dinner. On the way to the restaurant, his car had a puncture. He saw a light in the not too far distance. 'It's a gas station,' he told her. 'Lock the doors and I'll be back.'

The lights weren't those of any garage. They were of a roadside café. Jack, who can manipulate a piano keyboard with the brilliance of lightning, has never been so sure of more mechanical undertakings. He returned to the car feeling more than a little depressed – until he saw that Judy hadn't taken his instructions to heart. Instead of locking herself into the car, she had found the jack, hoisted her skirt as well as the chassis, and changed the wheel while her escort was away. She played her part in the film with equal ease.

It Should Happen to You was Judy Holliday's film from beginning to end, but she needed a sparring partner. Lemmon could have been just a foil. Instead, he was an inspired essential support. He, of course, gives *all* the credit to the slightly overweight, not-so-dumb blonde who had become a major star after just one picture, *Born Yesterday*. 'God, Judy was marvellous,' he told columnist Joyce Haber. He treated the whole thing as though he were doing poor Mr Cohn and his studio a great big favour. 'I really didn't give a damn about film,' he explained later.

However, *It Should Happen to You* sounded like an omen. Not only had he welcomed the chance of working with Holliday and Cukor, but a script by Garson Kanin and Ruth Gordon was not to be dismissed out of hand either. He thought, too, that he had all the answers with his agreement with Columbia. Unlike other stars in the studio era, he signed a non-exclusive contract, which allowed him to work not just for other Hollywood outfits, but also to do four plays on Broadway over the next seven years.

He didn't actually meet Cohn until after the film was completed. He had returned to New York at the earliest possible opportunity, but was called back because the studio needed some technical work done. That was when he went into Cohn's office and made the pilgrimage across the kind of carpet that all but covered his feet to the boss's desk. Cohn wanted Jack to change his name. 'If you don't change it,' he said, 'people will say the studio's a lemon.'

Jack couldn't be sure whether Cohn was trying to make a joke or not. In any case, he had his answer: did having a name like Humphrey stop Bogart being a convincing tough guy? And, what was more, who tried to call Walter Pidgeon a . . . pigeon? Jack tried very hard to convince Cohn that a Lemmon by any other name wouldn't act as sweet, but it took some persuasion.

The name that Cohn favoured now seems strange with twenty-odd years' hindsight of the Beatles' world-wide fame. Jack Lemmon, he said, would now become John Lennon.

Jack saw no reason to change. Besides, he said, it sounded too much like a Russian revolutionary's name.

'No,' said Cohn. 'That's L022en. I looked it up.'

Still Jack said he wasn't going to change.

'Oh yes you are,' said Cohn. 'Because otherwise, you're not going to be doing any more pictures.'

Jack was sufficiently riled to take that. 'Okay,' he said. 'I don't care. I'm going back to New York. I got a play. The hell with it.' He also made another point: it was a name, he said, that earned him a thousand fan letters a week. He then sent the studio head a letter in which he wrote: 'I'll grant you that my name isn't pretty, but then again, who can ever forget it – besides the public?'

Cohn had never been addressed like that before and he responded in the way of all bullies, by dropping his complaints. When the film was previewed, he liked it so much that he gave Jack even bigger letters than his contract specified for his name. He knew he had stumbled on a very big thing indeed.

It was the beginning of a fairly long relationship with Columbia, which was not everyone's idea of the perfect studio. Other outfits spent money as though they couldn't get rid of it fast enough. Columbia was so parsimonious that its studios were known as Poverty Row, and Harry Cohn had the kind of reputation that made all his rivals seem benevolent. On the other hand, he was a man who backed his hunches. It was he who turned an unknown called Margarita Cansino into every mogul's idea of a gold-plated meal ticket named Rita Hayworth.

It was he who took an idea rejected by every other major studio and had the biggest post-war musical success in *The Jolson Story*.

He had faith in Jack Lemmon and now that they had agreed that he didn't have to change his name – fortunately, no one knew about the Uhler part – he was going to work for him for their mutual benefit. Lemmon was now okay for Columbia. Ask Cohn who his favourite actor was and there was a good chance he would point to the newly hung portrait of Jack in the studio's gallery of stars and say 'my Harvard man' – as though Lemmon's education was in itself a plus for the studio. It was as if Cohn regarded himself as Jack's surrogate father, and all fathers had to be proud of their sons' achievements.

'I respected him,' Jack said. 'He never made me do a story I didn't like. But he did make *me* go tell the director and the writer that *I* didn't like it.'

But the studio boss tried all the same. He asked Jack to test for *Joseph and His Brethren*. The Lemmon philosophy was not to shout and say no, but to explain why it wasn't going to be sensible business either for the studio or for the young actor to take a role that was so patently unsuitable. But Cohn was insistent, and decided to use the velvet glove approach. His rival Louis B. Mayer would have collapsed in tears at this stage. Cohn simply asked Jack to do the test for him as a personal favour, as a sign of mutual respect. The voice was low. The pleas earnest.

'So,' Jack said, 'I go to the studio, put on a toga and thonged sandals and the rest, get my hair done and walk on to the set to test. And the whole crew broke up! I didn't even have to say anything. They just fell about when they saw me.' But he went through with the test, with more conviction than was wise, just to get the hell out of the sound stage.

It wasn't long before Cohn saw the error of his ways. 'Okay,' he said. 'You did me a favour. Now I'll do you a favour. I won't put the film of the test in the vaults. I'll burn it.' With the burning ceremony went his ambitions to film the Joseph story. It was never made.

Years after the mogul's death, Jack told *Variety*: 'I'm one of the few people who miss him. He was a giant. He could be an ogre and a tyrant, but he had good creative instincts.' Once, that is, he decided Jack wasn't going to play in the *Joseph* film.

While Columbia were coming up with ideas for Jack, who still wasn't sure he wanted to spend the rest of his days in Hollywood, Cynthia joined him in California. She was the practical one of the two. While Jack was totally engaged in forwarding his career, Cynthia had had to decide which came first – being an actress or being a wife. She wanted to keep on acting, but she valued even more being Mrs Jack Lemmon – even when he had not been doing so well himself. When, in 1953, she became pregnant, there was no doubt that the news was more important to her than any new theatrical contract could have been.

When the studio did come up with one, it was for a musical called *Three for the Show*, starring husband and wife dancers Marge and Gower Champion and Betty Grable at the tail-end of her career as a glamour symbol. Once more, it was Lemmon who got the best mentions from the critics. Everything pointed to his having made it in Hollywood in one easy jump. The offers of more films flooded in almost as frequently as the fan mail – from people who had seen his television shows and now delighted in the chance to view him on the big screen as well. He was beginning to worry about it almost as much as he was obviously delighted. It would be something that would dog him for years to come. 'We're happy,' he said, now that Cynthia was living with him again. 'But we don't want to stay in Hollywood for ever. Here, when you get successful, you get scared. You start protecting yourself. I don't want that. I want success in several media.'

Nevertheless he was firmly bedded down in Los Angeles, even if he wouldn't admit it. Later he would say: 'My motives in moving here were strictly physical – not cultural or social certainly. I never was much for a change of seasons. I perspire if I move my arm and I freeze easily. I've never enjoyed a coat and tie. I felt that out here I could breathe again and grow flowers and the whole schtick.' Jack was developing another characteristic. Brought up a Catholic, he was like other newcomers in Hollywood picking up the Yiddish ingredients of show-business language as easily as if he had been born on New York's East Side.

There was now a third Columbia film for him, and one where the biggest controversy of all was over the title. Finally it was

35

changed, although you would never know it. *Phffft* became *Phffft*. One 'f' less was considered sufficient to satisfy Columbia's front office, who were concerned about the saleability of a film with a name like that.

No picture called *Phffft* deserved to do anything but expire at the box office – but in fact the title did get people talking about it. 'What can it mean?' was supposed to be the question on everyone's tongue, and it was enough to ensure that the movie, in which Jack starred once again with Judy Holliday and the cool-looking Kim Novak, was a fair success. Jack and Judy, merely good friends in *It Should Happen to You*, were married in *Phffft* – except that their love was going the way of a spent match being doused in a saucer of water. Hence the title.

No one guessed that this was likely to happen again to Jack and Cynthia. Now ensconced in a small shingled house, like a Connecticut farmhouse, in the smart suburb of Brentwood in Los Angeles, they were frequently described in the gossip columns as one of the happiest couples in Hollywood. And when their son Christopher was born on 22 June 1954 they were both delighted. Soon after Christopher arrived the domestic scene was extended to include their Finnish maid, Impa, who when dinner was served would come out with announcements like, 'Eat, ready table.' She was, Jack used to tell friends, learning English at the same time as the baby.

On the home front Jack's one complaint seemed to be with the smog. He was becoming an active environmentalist, an attitude that would develop ever more strongly as the years passed. He was worried that his baby was beginning life breathing the equivalent of a carton of cigarettes a day – though he himself couldn't stop chain-smoking for Christopher's benefit – and they would go for long drives in the country. He and Cynthia lived a quiet life, and on Sunday mornings Jack would mess around in his garden like everyone else. Once a neighbour admired Jack's fuchsias. He had hit a soft spot, almost as soft as if he were to say that he had heard Jack playing the piano and where could he buy the sheet music. When Jack was asked about his magnificent fuchsias he played modest and didn't claim a great knowledge of the subject, but the following Sunday he was up early and over the wall into his neighbour's garden. The man was woken up by the noise of Jack's clippers. 'What are you doing?' he asked in amazement. 'Oh,' said Jack, 'I thought I'd do it for you. This is the time of year for it.' And he pruned the man's fuchsias for him.

After *Phffft* Jack took a comparatively small role in the musical film *My Sister Eileen*, playing the title character's personable brother. He was so charming in that film that you could call him cute, and matrons the world over took him to their bosoms. And not just the matrons. Jack's co-stars in the film, Betty Garrett and Janet Leigh, both told me they adored him, if not for his acting then for his piano-playing. For by this time he had established a tradition that no director worth his salt would dare break with: the sound stages had to have standing by not only Mr Lemmon's chair and Mr Lemmon's make-up but also Mr Lemmon's piano. He played it between takes, the rag doll bending even more as he remembered a phrase from his pre-Hollywood days, a cigarette dangling from his lips, a cup of coffee close at hand. 'Don't ever have your posture corrected,' Betty told him amid mumblings that the question mark would before long fall over and touch his toes instead of the piano keys. 'You'll lose your talent while they're doing it.'

The film took nine months to make, but because the dancing numbers were done first Jack only came to the studio towards the end. He and Betty Garrett had a good working relationship, mainly because they both took their work seriously – as well as having a sense of fun. As far as Betty was concerned Jack was the ideal leading man. He is, she told me, ' . . . relaxed and easy – but loves to rehearse, unlike most of the actors with whom I have worked. He'd say, "Do you want to go through that once more? Right. Let's do it."'

There was one scene in *My Sister Eileen* that everyone working on the movie remembers with undiluted affection. In the 'It's Bigger Than Both of Us' number, Jack was supposed to attempt to seduce Betty in between sips of brandy. At the end of the piece he was expected to throw his glass at the fireplace, Russian fashion.

Director Richard Quine, who had by now become one of Jack's closest friends and had appeared as an actor in the stage version of *My Sister Eileen*, was worried about doing it in rehearsal. Betty had to look shocked and surprised when the glass landed, smashing to smithereens, but Quine didn't think it a good idea to be quite so faithful to the final action when merely rehearsing. It would be a waste of expensive glass and the splinters would land where they shouldn't. 'What'll happen', said Quine, 'is that we'll place a mattress in the fireplace, and when the glass is supposed to break, I'll shout "Crash".'

Betty said she wasn't sure she could look shocked, perplexed and a bit frightened at the kind Mr Quine shouting 'Crash'.

'Don't worry,' said Jack in a whisper. 'When I throw that glass, I'll throw it.' The glass was thrown. It smashed against a wall and Betty looked as surprised as any director could have wished. 'Well, what do you know,' said Jack. 'The glass slipped out of my hand.'

As Betty now says, 'It was a very sweet thing to do. I almost had a crush on him. He was absolutely wonderful.'

For another number in the movie, 'Goodbye New, New York', Jack spent three days on the set – only to see the entire routine excised from the finished picture. 'I would have cried,' said Betty. 'All *he* said was, he was lucky to be in the picture at all. He took it all with such grace.' Jack was still at the stage in his career when he didn't complain too much – especially now that no one was allowed to suggest that he changed his name. Betty Garrett thought he had everything going for him.

Janet Leigh wasn't quite so conscious of the great Lemmon talent when he first went to work on the film. 'No one had realized how wonderful he was yet,' she told me. 'You could tell in working with him, though – although most of his scenes were with Betty. You could see what was inside. It took a little time for what was there to get out. When I was with him, it didn't show through yet. I certainly didn't know the extent of his brilliance. I did know there was something more than anyone had yet seen.'

Jack's fifth film role made rather more impact than he ever imagined. It came about because of that screen test he had taken on his first trip to Hollywood. Not the one that he passed, which led to his earlier film with Judy Holliday, but the one that he failed and which got Tyrone Power the job in *The Long Gray Line*. It was directed by the veteran Hollywood ace John Ford, taking a momentary rest from his Westerns and outdoor action films. Ford had positively refused to see the Lemmon test. He always said: 'No. I'm not gonna go with some twenty-seven-year-old kid. I want Ty Power to play it and that's that.'

Jack, however, always seemed to have friends in the right places, and one came to the rescue now. His name was Maurice Max, an assistant cutter at Columbia. He tacked on to the *Gray Line* rushes the Lemmon test – the one for which he had put up with every conceivable indignity, including having straws stuck up his nose before the clay was stuck on.

'What the hell is this?' asked the director and muttered a couple of the obscenities for which he was almost as famous as he was for his pictures. Now Ford was about to make the film version of what had been a huge Broadway success, *Mister Roberts*. It was the story of the fight between the officers of a Navy tugboat led on one side by the executive officer, played by Henry Fonda, and on the other by the captain, portrayed by James Cagney. The subsidiary role of the most junior officer on the ship, Ensign Pulver, was a vitally important one. He was the young fellow caught up in a man's world for the first time, ingenuously attractive but not really able to cope with all the politics. When Ford saw the *Gray Line* screen test, he said: 'He's lousy in this part – but he'd make a great Pulver.'

It was a hunch that paid off at about the time that Jack decided his curiosity had to get the better of him. He was itching to see how *The Long Gray Line* was shaping up. Eventually he had an opportunity to do just that, and he was on the Columbia lot when the movie was being shot on an adjoining sound stage.

It wasn't quite as easy to sneak on to the stage as he imagined. An elderly man wearing a black eye-patch and a shirt that owed more to long service than laundry bills approached him. 'You Jack Lemmon?' he asked. Well, Jack's Boston and Harvard background had taught him nothing if not to be scrupulously polite – especially when harmless old people look as though they are about to say something nice.

'Yes, I am,' he said, smiling widely, holding out his hand in greeting to the man whom he knew would have seen from the sidelines some of the real greats of Hollywood, a man who had probably been handling heavy equipment long before Fred Astaire or Rita Hayworth or even, perhaps, Clark Gable had ever seen a Columbia camera lens being focussed.

'What you doing here?' asked the old man.

'Oh,' said Jack, fumbling for excuses – he didn't want the ancient grip to get into trouble. 'I seem to have walked on to the wrong set.'

'Never mind,' said the man. 'You're a favourite of mine.' It was reason enough to be even more kind and polite. He muttered his gratitude for such pleasant words. But he wanted to get away. There wasn't a lot of time to spare, and he didn't relish the effects of upsetting an outfit where he had absolutely no business interfering.

'Come here. What you doing next?' Then before Jack could answer, the old man said, 'You ought to play Ensign Pulver in Mister Roberts.'

'Spread the word,' said Jack, who knew all about the role. It had overwhelmed everyone who had seen the Broadway play and was now being talked about in the Hollywood trade press; both Daily Variety and the Hollywood Reporter had carried stories about John Ford's imminent casting of the part. 'Yes, I should be playing the part,' he added. 'But no one seems to realize it.'

The old man's good eye twinkled. 'I'll show you an old Irish custom,' he said. 'You spit on your hand. I'll spit on mine – and we'll shake.'

It didn't seem all that hygienic, but again it was more polite to say yes than insult this obviously well-meaning man who had gone down hill.

They spat and they shook – and the old man said, 'I'm John Ford and you're Ensign Pulver.'

The part was perfect for him. Ensign Pulver got into the sort of scrapes that Ensign Lemmon could easily have been in. Jack found an empathy with the part right from the day he first read the script. 'Pulver's frenetic behaviour', he said, 'came out of his tremendous drive to prove himself to Doug Roberts ... and everybody else to be accepted.' If that was how he also saw his relationship with his own father, then he understood the part only too well.

It was to be Jack's first departure from Columbia. By this time, even Jack L. Warner had to agree that there must have been something in the close-to-rave reviews that this youngster Lemmon had been receiving. He agreed that, despite his past reservations, he should be taken on the Warner Brothers' pay-roll.

It was also the first demonstration of the power of the contract Jack had signed with Columbia. Other actors on long-term agreements with their studios were loaned out to rival organizations, but their original bosses kept the money they earned – which was frequently double, treble and even higher multiples of the amount they got from their original place of employment. Jack had had a clause inserted in his contract to the effect that the money he earned outside Columbia was his alone. As if to demonstrate the full meaning of that fact, he went to the Warners' cashier every Friday to collect his pay cheque personally. For years – until it became the accepted norm – others in the business wanted to know how he had achieved it. He said he didn't know. It was a deal negotiated for him by the William Morris Agency. 'All I know', he said at the time, 'is that Mr Morris always refers to it as the Jack Lemmon contract.' It was as though he had started a new disease that was now being named after him. As far as the big studios were concerned, he had.

Mister Roberts, the movie, was a sensational success. Fonda was good as the officer who is intelligent enough to know the responsibility he bears as the man whom everyone trusts. William Powell, in one of his very last roles, was elegant as the ship's doctor. Jack as Ensign Pulver was a delightful new phenomenon – and James Cagney was suitably obstinate as the captain.

James Cagney was, of course, best known as the tough guy of *Angels with Dirty Faces* and *Public Enemy*, the man who answered bickering wives with half a grapefruit smashed in their faces. But he was also a neat dancer. He had shown that talent in his early Hollywood days in *Footlight Parade*, as he had on Broadway. Then, in 1942, had come his favourite film *Yankee Doodle Dandy*, in which he played George M. Cohan. 'Once a song and dance man always a song and dance man,' was Cagney's slogan – and he showed Jack how to hoof a time step in spare moments during their evenings at the officers' quarters of the Midway base where they were all living.

He also gave Lemmon a lesson he has never forgotten: one of the most essential qualifications an actor needs for his craft is the power of observation. Jack told me, 'When we first met at the airport on the way to Midway, he said: "Are you still using your left hand exclusively?" I said, "What do you mean?" And he said, "Don't you remember you did that on a Kraft Playhouse about two years ago?" This one man caught it. He remembered that show.'

For Jack it was the supreme accolade. It not only made his day, but the trick of meticulous observation has stayed in his memory – as the Lemmon left hand had for Cagney – ever since.

There was one scene in the movie that will go down in film history along with Harold Lloyd hanging from the clock and Chaplin eating his bootlaces. In one hilarious moment of pantomime, Jack found himself in the ship's laundry as it was being blown up. He was smothered in a sea of soap suds. At least, that was the way it was supposed to look. In fact, real suds wouldn't have had the desired effect, so a chemical – and semi-toxic – substitute was used. It caused a severe skin rash and affected his eyes. For two days Jack had to take refuge in his bed; a stuntman who substituted for him for most of the shooting of that scene was much more seriously injured and was out of action for a fortnight.

An unexpected by-product of the picture was Lemmon's lasting success. From that moment on, he was in demand – and his price went up. The William Morris Agency were insisting on both more money and only very good parts. It meant that he either had roles that fitted his status or he would have to turn down work. The very success bred the threat of unemployment. He met the threat and beat it.

The film's acclaim nearly thirty years afterwards seems obvious. Yet not even prescient John Ford could have imagined how clever he was in getting Jack Lemmon. The Academy of Motion Picture Arts and Sciences obviously thought so – in 1956 he won an Oscar for the role as best supporting actor. It was an early demonstration of what the film community thought of him, and in show business there is no greater satisfaction than when you meet with the approval of your peers.

Jack Lemmon was no longer on his way. He had arrived.

4

You Can't Run Away From It

The *Mister Roberts* Oscar slightly alarmed Jack for another reason. Would the old gang off-Broadway still want him? He was still very attached to his New York friends, and felt that his success might upset them – that, after all, was why he had played the unemployed actor to them when he was doing regular television work.

At the time of the announcement of Jack Lemmon's nomination for the coveted statuette he made his first trip back to New York since leaving it for Harry Cohn. During the flight he tried to picture how it would be when he walked into the bar of Sardi's, an establishment he had never been able to afford before, and saw all his friends. When he arrived at Idlewild, he decided to go straight there and get it over with. When his friends saw him they shook his hands, clapped him on the back, and told him how proud they were of the local boy made good at the other side of the States. 'I sat there getting quietly mulled,' he told the *New York Times*. 'And, later, going down to the Players' Club, I congratulated myself all the way. "You're a great kid, Lemmon. That was a marvellous job you did in *Mister Roberts*. You're just a great little actor."' It was, after all, possible to succeed *and* have friends.

Jack was by all accounts a goldmine: the seams were bursting, and whatever came out was pure 24-carat. It was a dangerous situation full of forebodings, but one that Hollywood had faced before. The unacceptable face of the film industry was that it treated its stars as personal property and was prepared to ignore the consequences. While an actor or actress made money, there was little need to worry about whether he would still be doing so in the following year or two.

All the rules said that Jack's next film, *You Can't Run Away From It*, would be the beginning of the end of Jack Lemmon. The story was about an heiress who goes missing because she can't stand her fiancé, and falls in love with one of the reporters on her trail. The trouble was it had been used before – in *It Happened One Night*. And that had been done perfectly – which should have been a warning to Columbia. The lots of all the big studios are littered with the corpses of remakes that never remade it.

You Can't Run Away From It was a textbook case. It was directed poorly by former singer-actor Dick Powell with his then wife June Allyson in the lead. Powell seems to have been looking over both shoulders at the same time – at both his wife and the earlier film's director, Frank Capra. He copied his scenes (although without that certain indefinable extra ingredient) including the famous 'wall of Jericho' one where the reporter (Lemmon) hangs up a blanket to separate his bed from that of the heiress (Allyson). In the original film, it had been Clark Gable sparing the blushes of Claudette Colbert.

The exception to the rules was that Jack survived it all with his reputation intact. He wasn't allowed to show that he was a brilliant comic actor – the inept script and direction didn't give him a chance. But everyone was prepared to give him the benefit of the doubt. In fact, Frank Capra himself was more convinced than ever that before long he wanted to make a film with Jack. It was not to happen, although the veteran director broke a rule himself and visited the set of a remake of one of his own films to see how the baby-faced star was getting on in Clark Gable's pyjamas.

'I think – in fact I know – that Lemmon is one of our greatest actors,' he told me, 'and it was apparent to me seeing him on the set that he would be so. Yet even now I don't think we have seen him working to his greatest potential. He's done a great deal since, but, as I thought then, I still think he hasn't been stretched sufficiently.'

That is a decidedly minority decision. Every writer who met

Jack in 1956 when the film was made was convinced he had everything – and nobody mentioned his posture. His co-star thought so too. June Allyson describes him now as 'one of the most professional people I've ever worked with and with that marvellous sense of humour. The nicest thing, I think, while we worked on that film, was the way he always showed respect for everyone else there. He never would expect anyone to do anything he was not prepared to do himself. And Dick [Powell] loved him. They got on very well indeed.'

The story is, however, that Powell was very worried about Jack's effect on his wife, as if frightened that their proximity would take a romantic turn. He made sure, in all the ninety-six minutes of the picture, that Lemmon and Allyson never kiss even once.

If the audiences noticed, they didn't complain as much about Jack as some did about the film itself. For Jack it was all part of the pinch-me-if-I'm-dreaming syndrome. He still wasn't able to grasp the fact that he was not just good but good enough for other people to enjoy him, too.

'I've been so lucky I can't help feeling there must be a bomb around the corner,' he said again and again. In an interview, at the time of making *You Can't Run Away From It*, he put it like this:

'I'm frankly worried about the publicity. Maybe, it's too much build-up for a fast let-down. I'd rather take it a little slower. . . . I look in the mirror, what do I see: not Greg Peck. That's for sure. No Hercules, either. Remember I am where Clark Gable took off his shirt and you could hear girls' squeals from Maine, to California. Well, I wonder what'll happen when I take my shirt off. I don't think it'll impress anybody much. They'll just see a skinny guy with his ribs sticking out. No Clark Gable. Just me.'

He found it difficult to realize that that was precisely what they had come to want to see. Was it insecurity? Probably more not wanting to chance his luck; the same kind of superstition that makes actors refuse to whistle in their dressing-rooms or say the dreaded word 'Macbeth'.

He was beginning to worry, too, about being permanently tagged a comic instead of an actor. He had a profound respect for comics. There was a time when he thought he would be quite capable of delivering a Bob Hope-type monologue of contemporary gags – given the Bob Hope joke factory – at machine-gun speed. But that wasn't what he ultimately wanted to do.

Jack once said: 'It really bugs me when someone thinks I'm a comic. If I read about "comedian Jack Lemmon", I gag. That means I'm not an actor. If you're a comic and somebody comes up to you and says, "Be funny, make me laugh", you're supposed to knock him into the aisle with a brilliant remark. I couldn't do that if my life depended on it. . . . I'm more concerned with what people think of me as an actor than I am with how many tickets are sold at the box office. Not that I'm unconcerned with that. It's important and I wouldn't be around very long if they didn't sell.

'Basically, I think people should be concerned with those whose opinions they respect, rather than what the public in general thinks of them. If someone in my own industry considers me a fine actor, that means more to me than flattery from some Joe Blow who knows nothing about acting. The latter can be pleasant, of course, but it's not why I'm an actor. I want to accomplish something more than merely winning popularity contests.'

Now many others actors had thought that – it used to be the reason why they regarded the Oscar as so important, before it was translated into millions of dollars more coming into the box office – but few had explained it so articulately. And those words made official what he felt as he picked up his bronze statuette.

The serious Jack wasn't the usual image he showed the public. Most people were accustomed to hearing the chuckle, and girls being called 'sweetie', and gossip writers portraying Jack and Cynthia – to say nothing of two-year-old Christopher – as the Hollywood family who never stopped laughing. Of Jack's home life columnist Sidney Skolsky had so far only revealed that he liked sleeping in his underpants, in a huge French-provincial bed, and that before retiring he always had a glass of milk and two doughnuts, loyal as ever to his father's business.

But, as the title of his last film indicated, you can't run away from it, and the thing that Jack and Cynthia could no longer bear was that their marriage had evaporated. Strain between them had reached such a pitch that they now decided to divorce. It was, like the words in one of the tunes he played endlessly on his piano, just one of those things.

Long, long after the dust of it all had settled, he decided that he had probably married too young, and that went for most actors. 'I was terribly self-absorbed and it helped wreck the marriage.' But at the time Jack tried not so much to make light of the divorce as to accept it as inevitable. He told reporters – breaking up is not something that a big star can keep to himself – that it was bound to happen. After all, he added, both his parents and those of his wife had split up. The way it was told it sounded like some inherited disease.

What Jack *had* inherited from John and Millie was the intense belief that a parting of the ways did not have to include bitterness. When he suspected that Harry Cohn might be in the process of making Cynthia the villain of the piece, he insisted that she did not come out badly in the press. The old Harvard boy wasn't just laying down that he remained a gentleman, but that he still cared for her and didn't want to see any liberties taken with her reputation.

As far as the timing of the announcement was concerned, the Lemmons had taken Christopher very much into their mutual consideration. If they were going to split, and it was inevitable that they would, then they had to do it before the boy could become aware of any tensions and be psychologically hit by their break-up. So Cynthia moved out of their Brentwood home and into a Nevada hotel to establish her necessary residence in the state before it could grant her divorce. Jack moved out of the house, too, and into a Beverly Hills apartment he had rented. He took his Oscar and his piano with him.

Hollywood was a place that broke marriages as quickly and as easily as it made and broke careers. A contract with a big studio was as much an invitation for young women to jump into an actor's bed as it was for the actor to make an impact on cinema audiences – though that wasn't the way Jack saw it, and while married to Cynthia the question of infidelity hadn't occurred to him.

Jack liked his next film much more than most other people did. But everyone had to admit it was a departure. After *Cowboy* in 1957, no one could say that he was just a comic. It was a serious role about a cowboy who gets disenchanted with lassooing cattle for a living. 'It's mostly a heavy drama,' said Jack at the time when it was sensible for him to plug his latest film and say it was the best thing he ever did. What he liked about it was that it gave him a chance to show he could work in that sort of medium. The film was based on the memoirs of Frank Harris, the American man-about-town who seems to have done everything in a life that, told completely faithfully, would have been strictly X-certificate.

It gave him an opportunity to work with people like Glenn Ford, Brian Donlevy and Anna Kashfi, who was most people's idea of a sultry woman. The film was directed by the veteran Delmer Daves, and was, unusually, shot in sequence, which meant that since Jack was expected to learn to ride in the movie, he did just that, both on camera and for real. He hadn't enjoyed being on the back of a four-legged beast since his altercations with his pony as a small child, and he was no more pleased about it now. He was in the saddle continuously for more than a week – with a woman's sanitary towel strapped to his backside to ease the soreness. As part of the PR campaign, he even claimed he was considering buying a horse of his own.

Jack was more in rhythm with *Fire Down Below*, his second 1957 movie, for this was a marriage of his two loves – acting and music. He may not yet have proved himself to be the second George Gershwin, but nevertheless he wrote the score for the film and had the pleasure of seeing the sheet music on sale in the shops at a time when that was still a considerable part of the music business. He had knocked out a few tunes on a mouth organ between scenes, and the producer Irving Allen had liked enough of what he heard to want to use it. Jack was his usual modest self. 'I'd say that was apple polishing, wouldn't you?' he noted at the time.

Four years later he got his first cheque for music royalties – $17. Few had invested in the music of *Fire Down Below* – it was, after all, in the background and there were Rita Hayworth and Robert Mitchum in addition to Jack to distract their attention. But it did offer more than a modicum of satisfaction to the frustrated songwriter. 'I think it's fair to assume that it wasn't a smash hit,' he said soon afterwards. 'The best you can say for me is that I'm not a rock 'n' roll writer. I think rock 'n' roll is the lowest musical point ever reached. It's like telling a child that two plus two equalling four is all he needs to know about addition. Rock 'n' roll isn't actually music. Most of the guys who plonk those guitars use only three chords.'

Fire Down Below was about a group of people fishing in the Caribbean who have a highly predictable row over a woman (Rita Hayworth). Once more, the most notable feature of the picture was that Jack was broadening his experience, and wasn't suffering in the course of doing it. The work wasn't as easy as it looked, not even the more fun aspects of it. 'Making love on the screen is a pretty cold-blooded business,' he told the local *Port of Spain Gazette* in Trinidad. 'It is not so bad when you know the woman, but with a total stranger it's a helluva hard job.' Fortunately for him, he was getting to know Rita Hayworth.

He also got himself involved in what he found to be very pleasant romantic diversions of the kind he hadn't allowed himself since marrying Cynthia. Other members of the cast were shocked by some of these liaisons, including one with a lady who had a reputation gained in the days when Trinidad was a stopping-off place for the United States Navy. Either way, he doesn't appear to have come away from Trinidad with anything more than a few memories and a reasonable performance preserved on film.

London was another matter. He decided that, having come back from the Caribbean looking as though he had spent three months in a cave, he needed some colour in his cheeks and would benefit by using a sun-lamp. He borrowed one from Robert Mitchum and turned all the controls in the wrong directions. It was on too hot for too long and his skin came out in a series of horrible blotches. Work on completing the film at Elstree Studios was cancelled for several days and, at a cost of some £20,000, Mitchum and the rest of the crew were given an unexpected holiday.

While he was in London Jack went to a party at the home of Sharman Douglas, whose father Louis had been United States Ambassador to the Court of St James's. Jack was greeted at the door and asked by his hostess: 'Do you know Margaret?'

'Margaret who?' he asked. The question was splashed across the gossip columns of Britain's papers – and those in almost every other country in the Western world, too – for weeks afterwards.

Margaret who? turned out to be Princess Margaret, a close friend of the ex-envoy's daughter. Later Jack, trying to make amends, took the party to London's smartest night-club, Les Ambassadeurs, where he promptly emptied a bottle of whisky all the way down Princess Margaret's dress. He then escorted her back to Clarence House in a taxi. She seemed thoroughly entertained by him. It was plain old-fashioned Hollywood chutzpah, aided and abetted by his fondness for the bottle that enabled him to be so successful with everyone he met.

London wasn't quite sure what to make of the new sophisticated comedy introduced by Jack to their Cinemascope screens, but his women fans were legion. In fact, he had a certain amount of trouble keeping girls away from the door of his hotel room.

Jack, now making about £80,000 a year from his films, was concerned about that. 'I guess you could call me an actor's actor,' he said. 'Money in the bank doesn't mean a thing. What counts is being able to look back when you're washed up at sixty and taking pleasure in one or two things you've done.' No one, least of all Jack, could foresee what would happen that far ahead, but in 1957 he was still saying that if anyone called him a comic, he'd 'get mad'. *Fire Down Below* answered his need. 'I haven't got a laugh line all the way through,' he said with a touch of pride, as well as of gratitude.

Back in Hollywood, always on the lookout for a long-term woman, Jack met the actress Felicia Farr. She was seven years younger than Jack, an independent girl with a great sense of humour – something of an echo of Millie, which may explain why Jack fell for Felicia the way he did. At the age of fourteen she had modelled bathing suits to pay for dancing lessons. She had married at seventeen and before she was eighteen had given birth to her daughter Denise. Two years later she was divorced. Ask Felicia how she came to be such a strong personality, and she would probably say it was inherited from her mother – a woman who at the age of twelve had hitch-hiked from one end of America to another and who in old age would get into plumber's overalls and do repairs to the houses she rented out in Hollywood. But above all Felicia was an immensely attractive, golden-haired woman, and she sent Jack into paroxysms of wild delight. No

51

sooner had he met her than Jack knew he was as smitten as he had only been before with acting, or playing the piano.

He nicknamed Felicia 'Felish' or 'Farfel' – a Yiddish word for a soup garnish – and immediately took to her daughter Denise. 'Before I met Felish, I never got angry,' Jack said, looking back on that fortuitous meeting. 'I was all bottled up, constricted, emotionally. She opened me up. For the first time in my life I could get violently mad *and* I could feel an attraction that I had never felt for any human being. She is so alive, so open to everything. She drew me out of myself. She made me care – about poverty, about politics, about the rotten air we breathe.'

Meanwhile Cynthia was teaming up with the man who was soon to be her second husband, the actor Cliff Robertson, who had been with the Lemmons in the Old Knick days. John and Millie, while living their separate lives, were very upset over the divorce and by Christopher being pulled between his two parents. They felt they had handled the upbringing of their son better by staying together long after their marriage had evaporated.

However, success had done one thing for Jack: it had put him at ease with his father. He no longer felt that he had to prove himself to the older man, to make sure that his father knew that there were fine things in him, even if he did spill whisky down a princess's dress. Millie was just as happy about her son. But she was not away from her own problems. Once the Ritz-Carlton had made it clear that they were not prepared to turn their number-one bar into a cemetery, she decided to let them forgo her patronage and do her drinking at home – and alone.

Jack was now beginning to make a few mistakes in his career. It would have been remarkable had he not – after all, jumping all the way up a hill sometimes involves an occasional slip backwards. He was too intelligent an actor to allow that to happen too often or too permanently, but not everything was tremendously successful. The mistakes were *Operation Mad Ball* and *Bell, Book and Candle*. Jack had survived all that had happened before – and for the most part come out very much on top – mainly because of his agreement with Harry Cohn. He did have the freedom to choose his own material, and when he didn't like projects for which he had been chosen he simply had to tell the director and writer that he didn't consider himself suitable for them.

With these two films, his judgment left him. The first was better than the second – mainly because his old friend Richard Quine was directing and it benefited from the company of two totally unpredictable actors who could be quite as crazy as Jack himself, Ernie Kovacs and Mickey Rooney. It also featured a young lady called Kathryn Grant, who later became Mrs Bing Crosby. The saving grace of this story about American troops in Normandy facing the rigours of the service – the most rigorous of which was the ban on their establishing a form of détente with a group of Army nurses – was the relationship between Lemmon and Kovacs, who appear to get on together like a pair of small boys at a kindergarten.

They liked each other so much that when they were both offered *Bell, Book and Candle* both said yes without bothering to ask the right questions. The play had been a great stage success with Rex Harrison in the lead, and it looked set to win on screen. After all, it was a reunion of the old boys' club. Not just Jack and Ernie Kovacs, but Richard Quine directing again, and there would be the distinguished advantages of having James Stewart, Kim Novak (Novak and Kovacs was to prove difficult for some newspapermen), Hermione Gingold and Elsa Lanchester. What Jack didn't realize was that he was in the picture more for his name on the billboards than anything else. His part was tiny, quite the smallest of all the 'names' in the movie – and he was too gentlemanly to compete for attention with the other actors when he could have stolen a scene or two. The compensation was that he and Kovacs remained great friends. 'He was one of the most stimulating people I've ever known,' he said long after Kovacs' death. 'To this day, we still sit and talk about him. He had antennae out in every direction. He wouldn't just talk about his own work.'

Jack too was branching out. For the first time, people who had never had the chance to eavesdrop as Jack tinkered with the keys of an upright piano on the side of a film set were able to appreciate his music. A record album, *A Twist of Lemmon*, was released, and included Jack's own composition 'With All My Love'. He was later to joke that he knew of four people who had bought it. And he said that, if he did another one, he would concentrate simply on playing the greats – Cole Porter, Jerome Kern and his own idol Gershwin.

One of the reasons it didn't sell was probably because it tried to exploit his new fame as a movie actor, and not his undoubted talent as a musician. It fell between two piano stools. But everything else seemed to be running perfectly for him, and despite two disastrous films the public was still crying for more, still waiting in line.

Felicia seemed delighted to be in the front of that line, although no one could say that their relationship was anything but fiery. Other people in love spend their time hugging, kissing and giving each other presents. Jack and Felicia did all that – and more. Right from the beginning they had some of the most spirited rows Hollywood had seen outside a movie set. They had them in the privacy of people's houses and in the glare of public restaurants. Once, Felicia shut Jack out of a room. He was so angry that he pushed his hand through the door. Felicia would describe it as a typical demonstration of Jack's personality. 'He's a door slammer. It's an exit. That way, he has the last word.'

When I met Jack he told me what happened. 'It was one o'clock in the morning and we had had what you might describe as an argument. The door had opened for me and closed when I realized I wasn't through – there was more that I wanted to say. Only, she wouldn't let me back in and that got me mad.'

Felicia told *Good Housekeeping* magazine: 'He was shaking his finger at me and telling me off and backing up, all set for his big exit. Well, I fixed him. I walked him to the door, opened it, said, "Good night, I'll see you around," and closed it gently behind him. That's what irritated him.'

As Jack tells it, he kept saying in a calm, soft voice: '"Open the door, or I'm going to kick it down . . . open the door, open the door." I finally got so mad, I reared back and hit it. I thought I'd killed myself. My fist went kaplow! right through the plywood. Now my hand is stuck. Now I start saying, "Don't open the door! Don't open the door!" And she opens the door. I thought my hand was going to be ripped off at the wrist.' Felicia had the door panel framed and gave it to Jack as a present.

In those last years of the 1950s, it was reasonable to expect that anyone as close in their love-hate as Jack and Felicia would before long be marrying. Cynthia and he had divorced due to incompatibility and he was free in the legal sense. But he was holding back. His past experience – and that of his parents and of so many of the friends who had beaten him to the altar and back again – had made him very wary indeed. 'I'm not contemplating marriage at this point,' he said again and again. 'And Felicia isn't either. I'm happy with the way things have been happening.'

It also looked as though he had learnt his lesson about the kind of films to choose. *It Happened to Jane* was a better bargain – with the Lemmon repertory in truer form. Once more, Quine was directing and Ernie Kovacs co-starring. Doris Day was adding her girl-next-door appeal, and Steve Forrest played the smoothie who was a rival for her affection. To him, Jack Lemmon added a new dimension to pictures. 'Nobody suffers fools gladly, but Jack has a patience and approachability that allows him to feed on his contacts with people. He is interested in giving back to the public in a role what they can see as their personality. That's why he's always talking to people.' Jack impressed everybody on that picture, as he always did. But Forrest remembers another aspect that drew admiration. 'He was walking around in Boy Scout pants a lot of the time and everyone remarked on what wonderful legs he had!'

They did one scene together in a town meeting hall in Chester, Connecticut. 'To that point in my life, even including Anthony Quinn, I'd never worked with an actor who had that amount of energy,' Forrest told me. He seemed to use that energy verbally as well as physically working on the set. Forrest continued:

'I remember witnessing Jack's end of a telephone conversation he was having with Harry Cohn, who wanted him either to do a picture he didn't want to make or to work with an actress he refused to work with ever again. I heard Jack's end of the conversation, and I've seen some angry young bulls in my time, but nothing like this. Jack showed he had the temper, and the temperament, to say what he wanted to say. That wasn't done very often at that time.'

Jack and Kovacs got on beautifully throughout the film. This perfect partnership with another comic actor saw Jack blossom from light, baby-faced comedian (the description Jack resented so much) into a performer who could now only be described as an actor. *It Happened to Jane* wasn't only a turning-point in Jack's career, it was also an exceptionally happy film in the making.

Jack, Quine and Kovacs were sharing a seventeenth-century house complete with oak beams. 'At three o'clock every afternoon,' Steve Forrest tole me, 'Dick Quine would let us off for the day – whether Columbia ever found out I don't know. There was a beautiful trout stream nearby and the trout were absolutely teeming. So most of us would go trout-fishing. Jack wouldn't. He would go home and play the piano.' Anxious not to upset the rest of the household with his music, Jack had installed an electronic piano. The speakers could be turned off while Jack listened in on a pair of earphones, absolutely delighted at the arrangement, while nobody could hear a thing – not that they would have minded in the least.

Jack's performance in *It Happened to Jane* was noticed by one of America's most respected film directors, Billy Wilder. He specialized in the kind of film Jack should have been making, and he had had an eye on the actor for some time. Wilder said back in 1955 that Jack was the hardest-working actor in Hollywood. 'Whatever the role, he will research it to the bone, worrying it to the nub, doing the best possible job – and somehow making his expertise look instinctive. He is a thinking, highly inventive actor . . . he's somewhere between Chaplin and Cary Grant.' The only thing was that Wilder hadn't yet had an opportunity to benefit from that inventiveness himself.

By early 1959 Jack had made eleven films, and after *It Happened to Jane* he went briefly back to television to appear in a Playhouse 90 presentation of *Face of a Hero*. This was a play based on a novel by Pierre Boulle, who co-wrote *The Bridge on the River Kwai*, about a small-town prosecuting attorney who wears the face of a hero but who manages to convict an innocent boy of a capital crime in order to further his own career. The play received so much fan-mail that Jack decided to take it to Broadway the following year. But in the interim Billy Wilder stepped in.

Wilder knew what he was doing. He had an idea in mind: thirty years after Al Capone and the St Valentine's Day massacre he felt it was time to laugh at the Chicago gang wars. He wasn't suggesting turning all that blood and gore into slapstick. There were going to be two men dressed as women who get into bed with real women . . . but it was going to be very subtle, and that was where having Billy Wilder direct his own story was so important. It was clear when Wilder phoned Jack and offered him the role of one of the men dressed as women that it wasn't going to be *Charley's Aunt* in short skirts, or hostesses in a gay bar.

Jack and Billy had first talked about it a year earlier, in 1958. As Jack told the *Los Angeles Times*: 'I'm sitting in a little restaurant with checkerboard table-cloths and this guy comes over to me and says, "I'm Billy Vilder. I haf a picture for you. I'll call you in a year." A year later he calls and tells me about the part. I agreed to it, although he didn't have one word down on paper.'

All three of the film's stars – Jack (he was to be third in the credits), Marilyn Monroe and Tony Curtis – were signed before a word of his script was written. It contained an element of risk for both director and stars. For Wilder the risk was that his eminent reputation could be trampled in the mud by all those people who would see it as unpardonable pantomime. For Jack and Tony it was even harder: the mud in which they could be smothered could stick. For ever after it might be suggested they were very much at home in such a fairy story.

'*Some Like It Hot* for me was the turning point,' Jack told me. 'But strangely enough, everybody in town before the picture was made thought we were absolutely crazy. They thought that Wilder had lost his marbles. . . . Because how could you take two men like Curtis and Lemmon, two men in Hollywood, and dress them up in women's clothes for eighty-five per cent of the film? I mean, it's a five-minute sketch. It certainly can't be a film. Everybody in drag.'

Wilder wrote the script with his long-time partner I.A.L. Diamond. It was about two out-of-work musicians who dress as girls simply to get jobs – in an all-women orchestra. They are also on the run after having inadvertently stumbled on that little fracas in the garage on St Valentine's Day. The success of the movie depended both on Lemmon and Curtis appearing to find it hard to be accepted as females, but just about managing it, and on exquisitely funny lines delivered with all the seriousness of a declaration of war.

'All our young ladies are virtuosos,' says the band-leader.

'I tell you, Joe,' says Jack, 'they're on to us. And they're going to line us up against the wall and . . . then the cops are going to find two dead dames and they're going to take us to the ladies' morgue and when they undress us, I tell you, Joe, I'll die of shame.'

And when Jack tells the old roué millionaire (played by Joe E. Brown) that he can't marry him because he's a man, the suitor replies: 'Well, nobody's perfect.'

Another problem could have been the relationship between the male-cum-female stars and the overpowering all-woman magnetism of the band's vocalist, Marilyn Monroe, whose reputation spelt trouble. That Jack kept his cool while Marilyn wriggled her way into the train sleeper compartment, pushing her breasts into his chin, was as much a tribute to her acting as to Lemmon's ability to control a situation. It turned out to be just about the best thing she ever did on film.

For Jack it was a much more serious test. Wilder told me that he had a fairly good hunch right from the beginning that he would come through it with all pennants flying. 'I'd seen him on the screen in two or three pictures when he started and I knew there was a major talent on the rise, as it were, there and I had absolutely no doubt when he started working on *Some Like it Hot* that it would be good. I knew that one of the two men had to be Lemmon.'

As he puts it: 'There was something magical that happened. There was a *joie de vivre* about being in it. There was nothing campy in it. It was not satirical of women. It wasn't like *Tootsie* – a very good picture, but which got very philosophical. *He* just did it. If it was something that could be learned, I could have taught it to other actors, but what Jack did, he did because of his own unique talent.'

Wilder says he was certain it was going to work when he saw the costume tests. 'I went into the wardrobe bungalow – a caravan. It was the first time Jack and Tony were in their dresses and their high-heeled shoes and with their wigs on. I said, "Come on, let's go. The cameras are waiting for the tests."' That was when Tony Curtis thought he had met his doom. 'He just froze,' recalls Billy Wilder. 'He couldn't face being seen as a woman. Jack said, "Come on", grabbed him by the hand and dragged him out, like it was nothing. He demonstrated a kind of joy, asserting himself as the kind of multi-talented man that he is. There was only one other man who had this kind of joy of the profession, and that was the late Charles Laughton.'

It was the seriousness with which Jack treated the role that gained Wilder's admiration, as it had that of so many others. 'He made everything believable. You believed that he was a human being forced into that costume and putting on the airs of a woman without anything corny or unnecessarily camp. It wasn't forced humour.'

If the director thought Jack would be good in the part, he didn't prophesy just how good. 'He was very much better. It was like a composer who writes a piece of music and is very happy with it. Then, when he hears it played by Horowitz or Rubinstein, suddenly it becomes that much better. Every time you write something for him, it is so much better than what you give him. He's a thinking actor. He works at his lines.'

Every morning Wilder would be on the set at eight o'clock, ready to start work at nine. Jack would get there at eight-thirty. 'He'd have a cup of coffee in his hands and say: "You know, I've been thinking about that scene . . . I've an idea." If it was good, I'd just grab it. If it wasn't good, I'd look at him and he'd say, "Well, did you sleep well last night?" or "I didn't like it either." He was not like one of those so-called cerebral actors who would argue with you for hours.'

A simple statement that it wouldn't work was enough – which said as much about Jack's view of his own profession as his relationship with the director. 'Other actors argue for hours,' said Wilder. 'In the end, I say I am going to prove my point by filming their way and mine – which I do, without putting any film in the camera. With Jack, it's never necessary.'

It was Wilder's birthday during the shooting schedule of *Some Like It Hot*. The cameras were turning on the scene at the end of the picture, when the gangsters were gathering for their convention at the hotel in Florida where the girls' band was performing. They had rehearsed the scene where Edward G. Robinson Jnr jumped out of the cake and shot dead Spats, the gang boss played by George Raft. Wilder called 'Action' and faced the cake as the camera focussed on it. Except that this time, instead of the young hood appearing from inside the huge cake, a totally naked girl burst out.

'It was a birthday present for me,' recalled Wilder. 'Wasn't that sweet? It was Jack's idea, and Tony's.'

For Marilyn Monroe no film was easy to contemplate. This one was harder than most that had gone before it. She was pregnant at the time – though like her other pregnancies it was later discovered to be in a Fallopian tube and had to be aborted – and her husband Arthur Miller hovered round her like a cat protecting its young. Jack had a good relationship with all his colleagues on the film, including Marilyn. As Billy Wilder put it: 'He's incapable of saying anything mean or unpleasant about anyone. He's compassionate. He'll always find a way of saying something nice about other people.'

The nearest they got to a bust-up was when Marilyn took a fancy to Jack's flapper dress. As he later reported, Ory Kelly, who for years had been Warner Brothers' number-one costume designer and was known for his effeminacy, went into fits of anger when he found out. 'She took your dress! The bitch has pinched your dress!' There was nothing for it. Marilyn at the time was a bigger star than Jack, and if she insisted on wearing a dress that had been designed for him in the movie, then there was nothing for it but for Kelly to design a new gown for Jack. But Marilyn probably knew what she was doing.

'Marilyn had an absolute built-in barometer,' Jack told me, and went on, 'It took me about two weeks to kind of figure her out or get used to her. I adored her and we got on famously, but at first she just threw me. Marilyn, unlike any other actress I've ever worked with, knew what was right for her. And she would just stop, whether it was one line or five pages – and not wait for the director to call "Cut." She just said, "Sorry. . . . " We had one scene and something was bugging her. She had just those two lines – "Where's the bourbon? Oh, that's where it is." I kept betting Tony on which take she would get it. I think I lost about $15. Tony said, "I smell a thirty-take coming on." I said, "Oh no. Fifteen." That was five dollars. Then it was twenty – another five dollars. Then, twenty-five, still five dollars more. But Marilyn knew what she was doing. She was great and her instincts were right.' Sometimes she did as many as forty takes.

She was, he said a few months after making the picture, 'absolutely unpredictable. She simply isn't like other people. If we were all in the same building and it began to fall down, we'd all run. But Marilyn would probably run in a totally different direction. But the point is, she wouldn't get hit by any falling bricks because she's not only different, she's smart.'

In an interview with the *Chicago Tribune* in 1979 Jack said he didn't think she was very happy. 'I think there was always a lot of façade when her mood seemed to be gay. Underneath, I think she had been very hurt and by the time I worked with her I don't think she would let many people get close any more. When she liked someone, I think she'd let you get just so close and then a screen would drop because she didn't want to get hurt again.' But the worst problem she created on set was keeping everyone waiting. 'She was so late it became a pathological thing with her. She was incapable of leaving her dressing room. She drove Billy Wilder crazy.'

Stories that Wilder and Marilyn fought like cat and dog were greatly exaggerated. Lemmon recalled the director saying: 'With this girl, you may take a lot more takes than you think necessary, but when she's finally got a scene right, it's worth it.'

Tony Curtis, however, was less charitable about her. He was the one in the picture who dresses up as the Cary Grant-accented oil tycoon and falls madly in love with Marilyn. 'Tony had a much rougher time with Marilyn,' said Billy Wilder. 'They didn't get on well at all. They had had a series of run-ins before. But after their love scene, Tony said, "I'd rather kiss Hitler." Well, I'm not so sure.'

Jack has always said, 'All my life I've always wanted to be the best actor I can be. It is my greatest fortune, I guess, that I love what I'm best able to do.' *Some Like It Hot* was the perfect demonstration of that. 'It was by far the best farce script I'd ever read, even if everyone thought we were insane. Fortunately, it turned out to be an enormous smash. I just adore it. I think it's a classic job of writing and directing. It's Billy at his best.'

Jack played Daphne, Curtis was Josephine. In the film, Jack looks at his dress and says to Curtis: 'It's so draughty. They must be catching cold all the time.' As for his shoes, 'How do they walk on these things? How do they keep their balance?' Then he adds, 'I feel everyone must be staring at me.'

'With those legs,' replies Curtis, 'are you crazy?'

It was the business of making feminine movements and wearing those draughty, awkward clothes that presented the hardest problem. It turned into an athletic exercise as well as a *tour de force* of acting. So that they bulged in the right places, they wore all-in-one corselettes, suitably padded. So that they didn't bulge in the wrong ones, they wore jock-straps.

The easiest of the problems of playing a woman was having to shave regularly. Three times a day he and Tony would take out their razors, while the studio's insurance company hoped they wouldn't so much as nick their faces. Jack cut his legs once. High-heeled shoes were not so easy.

A female impersonator came over from Europe to teach them how to walk like women. It was a complicated exercise demonstrating that one foot is ever so delicately put in front of the other. After days of trying this, they gave up. Not because they couldn't manage it – hard though it was, actors that they were, they could. But it distorted the image they were trying to create. Daphne and Josephine hadn't had any training. They were simply two guys running away from the mob. Really men dressed up as women, they would simply be making the best job of it that they could – and if they got away with being two somewhat ungainly females, that's all they could hope for.

'At the end of three days,' Jack told me, 'the man quit. He said, "Curtis can be magnificent. Lemmon is hopeless."' It was typical Lemmon courtesy to remember it like that.

As Jack struggled with his high heels, he thought of his earliest success in life as a runner. 'I used to get what we call shin splints,' he explained to me. 'The tissue that is connected to the bone comes slightly separated from it and is terribly painful. It mostly affected the muscles at the back. Why women do it to themselves – let alone how – I'll really never know. But Tony and I suffered the tortures of the damned in those high heels, let alone got used to them.'

But both of them scored. They knew it the day they tried out their new 'bodies', their costumes and their walk for the first time before an unsuspecting public at the studio. It was the bravest thing they could do, but the only real test – they walked into the ladies' room and straightened their hair and adjusted their lipstick. Not one of the real women noticed anything particularly strange. Even their 1920s' dresses were regarded as what one might expect to see in a film studio.

Naturally both men were delighted – although first looks in the mirror could be unnerving, what with the heavy eye make-up and the cupid's bow lips. Jack looked at himself and saw – his mother. After a few days, he realized that unconsciously he was playing Millie, too. When he told her she saw it as great fun, which Jack took as an enormous compliment.

Every man born tries at some time in his life to imitate a woman. What he invariably does is to speak in a falsetto. Early on, Jack and Tony realized that wouldn't work – they had to go up one key and accentuate certain words, particularly the adjectives. It worked. They also had to adopt a whole series of mannerisms – and not just in walking and talking. They had to observe how women sat down, a wholly pleasant exercise, but one that was necessary for the success of their professional endeavours. They discovered that women 'don't just plop into a chair'. As Jack put it, 'You have to sort of melt into it.'

No one in the audience believed they were really women. But it had to seem reasonable that everyone else on screen would be taken in. Jack said it was like a suspense story where the audience knows who the killer is, but the guys up on the screen don't. Billy Wilder's term for it was a 'willing suspension of disbelief'. When real people did look twice at them it was merely to wonder how two women looking that dreadful could dare to go out in the open.

But the whole comedy exercise was exhausting. The sweat poured off the brows in *Some Like It Hot* much more readily than

63

it had in some of the more serious Lemmon roles. 'I think', he told me, 'that *any* form of comedy is more difficult to achieve than drama. And that's on all levels – not just the acting, but the directing and the writing, because the timing has to be minute. If a drama is flawed, it can still hold you. It will still grip you if there are key scenes that work or if a performance is interesting. But in comedy, the onus is on you.'

Once the cameras stopped rolling for the last time, everyone had a gut feeling that it had paid off. *Some Like It Hot* may have been one long series of clichés, older, as Jack said, than putting a lampshade on your head and pretending that you're a guy dressed as a dame. But Wilder's treatment of them made two hours and three minutes unforgettable. 'And,' Jack told the *Saturday Evening Post*, 'he did it on such a plane that, while it was a naughty picture, it wasn't a dirty or a vulgar picture.'

The studio's executives were not so sure. After the first sneak preview of the picture, they were incensed. They hated it. They thought it was too near the mark. At least fifteen minutes had to be cut. Predictably, Billy Wilder refused, then compromised by taking out thirty seconds. A week later, the film was previewed again – and this time you couldn't hear whether the offending lines had been taken out or not; for minutes at a time whole lines of dialogue were drowned by laughter from the audience.

It wasn't until *Some Like It Hot* was played before the public and the critics that Lemmon and the rest of the team knew for sure that they had a hit on their hands.

As Jack told me: 'That's the most frustrating thing about film. You can't do it again if you don't get it just right. If there's a director you can totally trust, you go along with him and that's great. You will never know whether a timing is right until it is run in a theatre before an audience. And then it's too late. In a live theatre, you can go out of town. You can try. If one night you give a certain reading and it doesn't work – or if you give a beat at a certain time before the punch line – that's okay because tomorrow you can have another crack at it. Then you can find out. Once you've found it, hopefully you can turn the key in the lock.'

With *Some Like It Hot*, the door opened wide for him. It was good enough for both Jack and Billy Wilder to get Academy Award nominations for their efforts. Charles Lang was nominated, too, for photography. *Time* magazine said of Jack in the movie: 'Lipsticked, mascaraed and tilting at a precarious angle . . . actor Lemmon digs out most of the laughs in the script.' As for Jack himself, he was walking tall – even without high heels. He could now be considered a major star.

Billy Wilder knew it and carried on building him up with all the enthusiasm of an art dealer who has found a painting everyone else knew was good but which he has a hunch is by an old master. Jack Lemmon was a young master of his own craft. If people wanted to compare him with Chaplin or Grant that was okay, but Wilder was sure that it wouldn't be long before other actors would be compared with Lemmon.

He now had a chance to disprove those old adages about lightning never striking in the same place twice. And it wasn't simply because *Some Like It Hot* addicts, who were rapidly turning the film into a cult movie, wanted more comedy from Lemmon. *The Apartment* was not strictly speaking a comedy, although there were times when Jack made audiences laugh, and it was a second successful collaboration.

One moment Jack was pouring forth some of the funniest one-liners ever heard on screen. The next he was trying to help the heroine, stretched out in bed after taking an overdose. It was an early example of how Jack Lemmon could make the trip from comedy to tragedy in one breath – or from one frame to the next. His co-star was Shirley MacLaine, a young woman who drove Billy Wilder frantic by her habit of ad libbing her own dialogue – to say nothing of a marked reluctance to rehearse. 'We got used to her,' Jack told *Variety*, 'because mainly she's a helluva gal.'

He himself related perfectly to his own character – a man who constantly needed a nasal spray, even if there was a time when it was directed in Fred MacMurray's eye. MacMurray, his boss, asks him: 'Tell me Baxter, what is it that makes you so popular? . . . There's a certain key floating around.' The key didn't just fit Baxter's apartment. It also opened the door to keeping Lemmon in employment.

It was again Wilder's own story, about a very junior member of an office staff who ingratiates himself with his boss by making his apartment available for the entertainment of lady friends. Other people in the office benefited equally from his generosity, but the real winners were the audiences. Jack didn't see the script till Billy was ready to start filming, and it took him a long time to 'get' the character he was playing. 'When I finally got him,' Jack said years later, 'I felt a great deal of sympathy, a great deal of empathy, for him. I was actually worried that it would be dull or lacklustre, that I would be behaving, not acting. It sounds conceited, but I was afraid that possibly I had done too good a job – that I had been too honest.' He rarely worried about doing too good a job. He always feared that the job he did might not have been enough to tell the story that should be told.

When the film was finished, Wilder and Jack went off to Europe to capitalize on the fact that they had, to use the director's version of the adage, 'caught lightning in the bottle twice'. They took *The Apartment* to France, to Belgium, to Britain, to Germany and to Denmark. 'That, of course, was marvellous fun,' Wilder recalled. 'It was lovely going with him because I felt I could show off.'

Not revealing his knowledge of the architecture of Paris or London or Copenhagen, he wasn't showing off *to* Jack. He was showing off *Jack* to the Europeans. 'You know, there is such a thing as the beautiful American,' he told me. Jack was particularly moved when Wilder showed him his birthplace in Vienna. Together, they also went to East and West Berlin. Billy didn't mention his own escape from Austria or the fact that he had lost his family in the holocaust.

At the Dorchester Hotel in London Jack was tickled by being given what he called the 'Maharajah's suite' – marble, real grass on the terrace and an assistant manager in tails at two o'clock in the afternoon. 'I enjoy things like that.' He also enjoyed the company of Billy Wilder. It was very much a case of mutual admiration. 'Working with Billy', he told the *New York Times*, 'has been the greatest experience of my life. Billy lacks Hollywood's widespread inability to make a decision, and he won't compromise to save a nickel.'

Once more Jack had his mother in mind while making the film. The lonely woman in a bar in *The Apartment* made him think about her. He could understand a woman who liked to be thought funny but whose only good friend was a bottle of bourbon. If anyone doubted that he was affected by his own part, the drawn expression on his face and the heavy eyes were those of a man who can't easily escape it. 'I *do* live a part,' he said once. 'That little schnook was me nights and weekends, too.'

But it earned him a sort of immortality. Soon after the movie, Jack and Shirley were invited to place their hand and footprints in wet cement at the entrance to Grauman's Chinese Theatre, the 141st and 142nd stars to do so.

The picture earned Jack and Billy Wilder Oscar nominations. Billy won twice: he shared the Writer's award with his partner I. A. L. Diamond, and won the Oscar for the Best Director. Jack won nothing at all, apart from the certificate that said he had been nominated. He also won the admiration of virtually everybody who saw the picture. It was a tremendous success at the box office and it confirmed Jack as a highly marketable commodity.

If he needed bringing down to earth, it was Christopher – in the way of all small boys – who did so. 'Gee, Dad,' he said soon after the première, 'I just met someone even older than you.'

The Wackiest Ship in the Army, the other 1960 Lemmon release, was much more in the earlier mould – pure comedy with a touch of *Mister Roberts* about it. After the great hurrahs for *Some Like It Hot* and *The Apartment*, it was almost reasonable to think that this was now going to be the norm. It wasn't like that, although this story about a sailing ship falling to pieces in the South Pacific, while managing to upset the Japanese Empire, had a lot of nice touches about it. But no one could pretend it was an important milestone in the Jack Lemmon career – other than helping him fulfil his obligations to Columbia.

What concerned him more was his relationship with Felicia, although their friends were fed up with their not coming to terms. Cynthia's marriage to Cliff Robertson had broken up after an unpleasant divorce, and now the gossip columns were suggesting that she and Jack would get together again. It seems that Jack started the rumour quite accidentally by saying: 'Wouldn't it be wonderful if Cinnie and Chris could come over and visit me?' What he meant was that he wanted to be with his son, but it was convenient to read more into it than that. What he finally wanted was partnership with Felicia. It might be described as stormy, but it was a summer storm. As far as he was concerned, there was more often sun than cloudbursts and the magnetism they felt for each other was on both poles. They both decided they were in love, but that was as far as it went. Jack had his career, and six-year-old Christopher took a lot of his spare time; Felicia too had her acting and her eight-year-old daughter Denise. If Jack did decide to get married, it would have to be sandwiched between acting commitments. Film scripts were thundering on to his doormat with increasing rapidity, but he still harboured ambitions to show he had been right when he said that real acting was on the stage of a Broadway theatre, not in front of a camera on a movie set. Now was the time, he decided, to play New York.

5

Days of Wine and Roses

Face of a Hero on stage turned out to be a bitter disappointment, both for Jack and for his admirers. He had had faith in it all the way from the television studios where he first decided it would transfer beautifully from the small screen to the proscenium arch. People told him that he needed his head examined. The golden boy of Hollywood was risking his career on a proposition that was anything but gilt-edged.

But he had a double interest in pursuing this autumn madness – the play was to open at the Eugene O'Neill Theatre on West 49th Street on 20 October 1960. He not only desperately wanted to get the feel of the boards beneath his feet, but also to prove to the Hollywood moguls that he was more than a business investment to them.

It was a familiar symptom of star disease. Jack was mercifully immune to most of the others – the prima donna behaviour, the demands for special consideration, the insistence on new Cadillacs and other fringe benefits, the refusal to be nice to the press or the people who made him, the public. But he displayed examples of the infection that had been known to strike other people – the feeling that what he was doing wasn't a real demonstration of his art.

Jack said much the same thing when he sat on the stage of the Walnut Theatre in Philadelphia, before being 'thrown out'. 'I wanted to use my muscles again,' he said. 'I'm a better actor already, after just three rehearsals – and if this play bombed, I'd do it again tomorrow.' Bomb, the play did – and as Jack said: 'They threw us out of Philadelphia and only let us stay in Boston because I was a local boy.' It was a blow to his ego, for it proved that the stage, which he still claimed to be his first love, was less kind to him than the studio. Perhaps it was because he had so easily triumphed in Hollywood that he was unwittingly devaluing the importance of his screen success.

'My problem', he admitted, 'is that I want to play every part better than any other actor could ever play it. Now I know this is a form of egomania, but I also think that if you are *that* serious about your work, it drives you to your best performance, not just a competent one all the folks will like.' That statement to the *New York Times* said a great deal about his attitude to his talent – recognizing that he had it, but frightened that his use of his abilities would be mistaken for conceit.

Things had gone wrong from the beginning. Long after the first script conferences and casting sessions were held, the leading lady – who played Jack's wife – was changed. Betsy Blair, a successful Broadway and Hollywood actress, was brought in to take over. She was a friend of both the playwright, Robert L. Joseph, and the director, Alexander Mackendrick. Mackendrick had achieved a number of screen successes, notably the brilliant Burt Lancaster and Tony Curtis picture *Sweet Smell of Success*, but *Face of a Hero* was his stage début. He may not then have had the authority of the film direction Jack was used to taking. At any rate the rehearsals didn't go smoothly and it was clear to anyone who knew Jack that his usual buoyancy and confidence were lacking.

The play had already been in rehearsal for some time when Betsy joined the company. She rehearsed with Jack's understudy because everyone else was much further ahead than her, and on top of this her part was totally rewritten and she was turned into an alcoholic. By the time the play went on the stage the alcoholic element had been taken out again, leaving Betsy with little time to get into the character properly. 'None of us felt that the play was working,' she told me afterwards. 'Jack suffered a great deal.'

Jack tried not to show too much of his frustration. He attended the various functions in Philadelphia and Boston to which he had committed himself. Nothing would persuade him to let down people who had expressed faith in and friendship for him, and after a ladies' luncheon at which he looked grey and exhausted he returned, dealing with a gang of autograph hunters on the way, to the Walnut Theatre for final rehearsals. At one o'clock the following morning, after going for the last time through the latest rewrites, he could be seen looking up at the dark sky and muttering, 'Oh God, I want my mother – and my agent.'

'He was very nervous,' Betsy Blair remembered. 'He wasn't frenetic. I think he felt that it was the first play he had done since his enormous success in Hollywood and wanted to do it well. My impression of him was that he was terribly intense, impatient with himself. He was perfectly mannered and well behaved.'

Felicia was with him much of the time, encouraging him from the sidelines, yet the play was all-consuming. These weren't the times he had enjoyed at Columbia or Warner Brothers when he could unwind and enjoy the company of his fellow actors. Betsy Blair doesn't even remember his playing the piano in offstage moments, which may have said a great deal about the way the play was going. He wasn't the bundle of fun he seemed to be on the West Coast. 'He was charming and nice. But maybe because nobody was happy with the play, it didn't work out so well.'

Jack would have had good enough reason to plead for both his mother and his agent after reading the first-night reviews, both in Philadelphia and later in Manhattan itself. Howard Taubman in the *New York Times* said: 'Egg splatters the *Face of a Hero*, which opened at the Eugene O'Neill Theatre last night. Some was flung by intent; a great deal more landed inadvertently, thanks to the ineptitude of the playwright.' As for Jack Lemmon, '. . . a pleasant young man, who has been a tremendous success in Hollywood, has no chance . . . to show whether he can act in the theatre. . . . He talks but does not reveal himself. There is less conviction in him, even at the end when the face of the "hero" is bared, than in a paper tiger.'

The sting was to get worse and the barbs more severe. 'How so many people of good repute got into this misadventure is one of those Broadway mysteries. Alexander Mackendrick, who has notable films to his credit, is responsible for the direction, such as it is . . . Albert Dekker, James Donald, George Grizzard, Russell

Collins and Roy Poole crash through the fog of the play to prove that they know their business. Betsy Blair . . . speaks in a loud monotone and Frank Conroy as the dean seems to be as embarrassed by his lines as we are for him.'

Jack tried hard not to be daunted by all this. It was a play, he was to admit, 'which the audience couldn't understand, I couldn't understand. In fact, none of the cast could understand.' Three years later, he was still trying to analyze what had gone wrong with it and coming to much the same conclusions, although his comments were somewhat more severe. 'I never found the hero,' he told the *Chicago Tribune*. 'I couldn't find the hook. The play wasn't well written in the first place, but my performance didn't help one damn bit. I was off the stage about three or four minutes in the entire play. I lost a couple of pounds a night. If it had been a hit, I would have been a wreck.' It sounded funny, but even Jack couldn't let that go. 'No,' he corrected himself, 'that's not true. If you've got something good, it's a different kind of exhaustion. You're drained at a different level.'

Jack had been one of his own 'angels' in the play, investing money in it as well as energy and talent. The financial side of his endeavours benefited from a fair number of advance bookings from out-of-towners who arranged coach parties to take them to Manhattan for the night. There the play ran for the thirty-six performances for which Jack was contracted, and despite the reviews ticket sales never dropped to the point where the Eugene O'Neill management considered taking it off. But as soon as Jack's contracted time was up the play quietly folded. With his usual humour struggling to the surface Jack swallowed his disappointment, and took to calling the play *Trace of a Zero*. 'But I'd do it again in a minute,' he said afterwards. 'Trying to figure out how to make a sick play go is a painful joy, but it's a joy.'

He was to have that pain and that joy again. But for the moment he was concentrating on going back to Hollywood. And to Felicia. Their mutual opposition to marriage was beginning to weaken, though neither was yet in a mood for commitment. It wasn't that they were still constantly quarrelling. Their fights were the kind that earned them the title of lovebirds from most of their friends. They would shout, drive away from each other's homes, slam doors – and then phone for an opportunity to make up. When they made up, they were the envy of all around them.

Meanwhile, Millie made occasional visits to her son's four-room cottage in Bel Air high above Beverly Hills. When he came, she made him a stock of frozen dinners as a standby when he wasn't taking Felicia or business companions out to eat at local restaurants. But it was in his own back yard, dressed in a sloppy but expensive cashmere sweater, that he could relax best. It was necessary for him to go to a few regulation Hollywood occasions – like film premières – but, on the whole, he preferred to stay at home. His work was exhausting and he needed to be able to unwind. When he went to a night-club – although he wasn't averse to attending the odd drinking party – it was usually more for the cabaret than for an evening out. Every so often he would throw a party for perhaps up to forty guests, normally serving Chinese food. The star attraction at these shindigs was Jack himself, playing his piano. Sometimes favoured guests would be invited out on to his patio to study the stars through his telescope – although one observer suggested that as his house was so high up in the mountains a reading glass was all that was necessary.

When he returned from the fiasco of New York Jack didn't need a glass of any kind to see he was still very much in demand. Now that he had a flop behind him, he needed to prove that he could still keep the customers enthusing over his work. And the parts were flooding in – with Jack given every opportunity to do only the roles he would enjoy and which would stretch his talents. But it wasn't easy. 'After one smash,' he said at the time of the Broadway failure, 'you must be sure that your next picture is just as important. When you get into your thirties, you can only afford to accept the best scripts offered to you, and the other conditions have to be right, too – good writing, good directing, other stars in the picture. If you defy the system – take a character role occasionally, as many fine actors do in England – then you're not a star any more and the best pictures, the best scripts, won't be offered to you.'

Jack had put his finger on it. In an incredibly short time, even by Hollywood standards, he had gone from dreaming of getting work as an actor to getting a speaking part and becoming a character player, from wanting an occasional lead to hoping he would become a star, and then hitting the very top of Hollywood. 'What I did not realize, what never entered my mind at that point, is that when you become a star, you cannot act. You put a dime under your pillow and dream about great parts. You get them and then you suddenly find you're limited.'

So he was being exceedingly careful. In 1961 he took out an insurance policy – called Fred Astaire. No one would suggest that his motives for making *The Notorious Landlady* were simply ones of safety, but there was a lot to be said for the fact that Fred Astaire, even at sixty-two, was usually a first-class recipe for success in a movie. 'I marvelled at his perfectionism,' Jack was to tell me. 'That grace of movement. Wow!' For his part, Fred told me that working with Lemmon was good enough reason not to retire.

The picture was yet another directed by Richard Quine, who was as much Fred's friend as Jack's. The mutual regard he was able to foster in this story of an American diplomat in London was one of the great bonuses in the picture. Another was the giant-size pool table brought on to the set. It not only kept both Jack and Fred happy, it provided a chance for Astaire to move in a way not unlike his old dance routines. There was also the inevitable piano, which Astaire liked listening to as much as Jack enjoyed playing it.

Jack was Fred's assistant in the picture, but his role was scarcely a subsidiary one. Most of the story revolved around his affair with the notorious landlady, in the shape of the willowy beauty, Kim Novak. The lady had got herself involved in a murder mystery.

She also found the part slightly difficult. The English accent she had to adopt got her tied in knots. Richard Quine told me that only Jack could have eased her way through the picture as he did. 'I can't think of any other actor who would have been as tolerant and understanding and patient as Jack. He was absolutely marvellous. They were seemingly innocuous things – like making a comforting joke at the right time. He was never commiserating to the degree that it would seem he was being condescending, never that. He had the gift of always pretending that there were never any problems.'

The thing that delighted Londoners most was when the stars tried to get through the gates of Buckingham Palace for a scene. They were quickly escorted away. The film was intended to look as though it were shot exclusively on location in England, but most of it was filmed in America, on the Monterey peninsula. Jack didn't have much to say about the picture during the making. 'I don't know about the script,' he said. 'But the wardrobe is great.' It turned out to be a fair judgment on the picture. Pleasant to watch – aided by Astaire and Novak – but not one likely to go down in the annals as vintage Lemmon.

'Both Jack and I were under contract to Columbia,' Quine explained, 'and we were constantly trying to find projects that would wipe another one off our slates, so that we could get on with more fruitful things – because our contracts were not that lucrative. Every picture we made meant one less we would have to do at Columbia. We were searching for projects that would get rid of our commitments. That was one of them.' Their friendship made working together easy. As Quine said: 'We've played pool together, we've played golf together, we've dated together. . . .'

As always now, Felicia was watching Jack at work, but still they couldn't tie each other down to any serious decision about their future. It maddened their friends, frustrated the columnists and gave their families a certain concern. But emotionally it was a difficult time for Jack even without his doubts on the romantic front. A tiny part in *The Notorious Landlady*, a dapper, elderly man wearing a dark suit, a homburg hat and the kind of spectacles that give a man authority, was given to John Uhler Lemmon II, who had now moved to California to be near his son.

They were having, Jack was pleased to recall years later, great fun together. Giving the elder Lemmon a small part was an idea Jack knew his father would appreciate. Jack also had another job for him – chairman of the newly established family business, Jalem Productions, Jack's own film company. Making him head of the firm was a gesture that showed that Jack, at last, felt there were no barriers between his father and himself. Except that there was also a deeper reason. The senior Lemmon was dying of cancer.

In the meantime Jack was trying to ensure that the relationship with his own son was as close as he could wish. It wasn't. He had all the problems that an absentee father has to learn to expect. The ease that he liked to think existed with Christopher had gone, there were notable tensions when they met, which was only on set days at Jack's home, and that alone stiffened the atmosphere. Christopher had always lived with his mother, but the star craved every opportunity he could get to be with the boy. They played in the swimming pool and Jack taught Chris how to use the new snorkel equipment he bought him. In a rare moment of candour Jack admitted: 'It takes me a day to recover from Chris's visits, but I wouldn't miss them for anything.'

Jack's idea in setting up his own company was to make sure he was in a position to demand the best of both worlds – commerce and movie art. He even signed an agreement with Columbia to work for them for another three years. But it wasn't going to be an extension of the kind of contract from which both he and Quine had been anxious to escape. Now he would make just three films between 1961 and 1964 on a one-picture-a-year-non-exclusive basis. He said he wanted to be free to do things he fancied doing, not those that a studio wanted him to do. 'I want to be free to do . . . a stage play if the right one comes along.' He was booked solid to the end of 1963, so he had few worries on that score.

There was little hope that he would go back to the medium where he began – television. 'I am ashamed and disgusted with television,' he said in one interview. 'It used to be a medium you could be proud to appear in, but it's come down so far it's almost impossible to find a decent script, or at least one that the sponsor will let you put on.' It was a recurring theme. Anyone who didn't know Jack Lemmon could be forgiven for thinking that coming to the surface was some hidden grudge against the hand which had once fed him. He even told *Variety*: 'TV stinks! It's narrow-minded. What they've tried to do is the lowest denominator. They don't try to sell entertainment, but products. They're not concerned with how good a show is or can be, but how broad an appeal they can get to have audiences look at their commercials. It's a disease in the home.'

Setting up his own company was very much an economic proposition. He was paying ninety per cent of his personal income to the Internal Revenue Service. A company would only be taxed at a maximum rate of forty-eight per cent, and he would be allowed to write off all the expenses of getting a movie off the ground. Of course he couldn't use the money in the company as spending money, but it meant he could afford to do things he wanted to be able to do professionally.

His father's role in the company was not a long-term engagement. In March 1962 the recently retired Vice President of the Doughnut Corporation of America died in a hospital at Santa Monica, and was buried in Maryland. The day before the funeral Jack spent the night in a room over the funeral parlour, owned by an uncle. He went down into the mortuary room and spoke for a while to his father's coffin. When he came to leave he discovered that the only way he could get out again was through the street door. Once more, Jack was caught in a public thoroughfare wearing nothing more than a vest and a pair of underpants. Just as nonchalantly as before, he rang the bell in the middle of the night and walked upstairs. His father, he said, had 'lived long enough to see that things worked out. He was so pleased he'd sweated all the years of nothing with me.' With John Lemmon gone he treasured the relationship he had with his mother all the more. She still drank quite a lot – but she was also a bundle of laughs. Millie moved to California so they could see each other frequently, and Jack could drive over to her apartment to pick her up at weekends.

It was a time for reflection, but Jack had no time to pause for it. He was in the middle of a picture that required all the attention he could give. For now there was no blurred line between comedy and drama. *Days of Wine and Roses* was a harrowing part and the laughs were mostly from people who felt compelled to smile whenever they saw Jack on screen, looking as if he were in trouble – and it was an accepted thing that few people got into more trouble than Jack. The part was, however, a rehearsal for all that was going to follow, a preview of the Jack Lemmon that would excite new audiences with *The China Syndrome* and *Missing* a generation later.

For the most part Jack's great skill was in picking the roles that he knew he could play. In *Days of Wine and Roses* he would co-star with the very beautiful Lee Remick. It was a *ménage à trois* love story. The third person was the bottle. The film took almost two years to set up. *The Lost Weekend* apart, Hollywood had made up its collective mind not to make films about alcoholics – for so many people in the film capital, it was a subject too close for comfort. 'And while I was hanging around waiting, I found a part of me breathing a sigh of relief,' he said later. 'Maybe the film would never get going and then I'd be let off the hook. I found I was saying to myself, "Listen, you might not be able to play the little mother – so leave it alone. Go back to your comedies, they are easier and you can handle them."'

That wouldn't have been Jack Lemmon at all. Despite the objections and opposition, he had found a way to break out of a very comfortable straitjacket and he was going to do it. He was scared, but he was more determined than ever to succeed.

Both stars in the picture were in love with the grape as much as they were with each other – except that the husband was more willing to admit to the fact than was his wife. It was a situation that both saw for a time from the inside – by attending meetings of Alcoholics Anonymous, an organization that featured widely in the film. Jack and Lee went along and sat at the back unobtrusively. What disturbed Jack was that the membership thought he fitted in so well at their sessions. They spent several nights, too, in 'drunk tanks' studying people suffering from DTs and watching the effects of seeing pink elephants and other hallucinations experienced by hitherto unredeemed alcoholics. 'It was painful,' Jack said, 'but beneficial.'

In one scene in the picture Lemmon the alcoholic had to be strapped to a table. It was an idea he had suggested to the director, his friend Blake Edwards, after seeing it happen at one of these sessions. 'I saw a guy who was strapped down coming to, wondering what had happened. You're strapped down like you're a madman and you don't know why. God, it's so degrading. But it's also terribly dramatic, as opposed to just sitting on the floor of the tank.'

He could use a little comedy as well. He suggested – and again Blake bought it – that it could come in the scene where his character gets out of a taxi as loaded as a ten-ton truck at the beginning of a day. It seemed a good idea to lighten the mood before the big tragic scene – when he wakes his baby and then breaks down himself and cries. He walked straight into the plate-glass window of his home. It was a tragic scene, but it legitimately made people laugh at the same time. It was a scene – and an idea – which showed that Jack was very much in control of the situation. Perhaps its greatest significance was that he was able to marry the two disparate worlds of heavy drama and comedy without risking any further suggestions that he was, after all, *just* a comedian.

Days of Wine and Roses had begun as a television play produced by Warner Brothers. It starred Jack's old colleague – and successor as husband to Cynthia – Cliff Robertson, and Piper Laurie. Bill Orr, head of television at Warners, thought it would make a good feature film for the studio and suggested Jack Lemmon for the role. His father-in-law, Jack L. Warner, was sent a kinescope of the play – a primitive form of television recording, long before the use of tape, in which a film would be made direct from the 'tube'. The picture was dark and the quality generally abysmal. Jack Warner had an antipathy to stories about alcoholics. When he saw the kinescope, which was anything but hi-fi, he knew he was right in turning the offer down flat.

'If you're going to make another picture about a load of drunks,' he told Orr, 'forget it. Anyway, what I saw was terrible. Terribly gloomy.'

But a week or so later Orr had a phone call from his father-in-law. 'I've just read a wonderful script,' he said. 'And we're going to do a deal with William Morris. It's great. It's called *Days of Wine and Roses*.' It was the old story – the big mogul only wanting to do projects if he could persuade people that he had thought of them first.

The film was originally to be made by Twentieth Century-Fox, but at a time when that studio was still licking the wounds inflicted by the costly epic starring Elizabeth Taylor and Richard Burton, called *Cleopatra*, they thought better of it. Warner Brothers were not to regret their decision to walk where Fox had feared to tread. Twentieth Century-Fox were not the only studio to have considered the film. Jack, his producer Martin Manulis and the director Blake Edwards had hawked the film round practically every film company office in Hollywood. One by one, they turned the idea down. As Jack later reported, they all said the same thing to him: 'Aw, Jack you don't want to do that. Do a nice comedy. We'll do any comedy you want. But don't do that damned downbeat thing. Who's going to care about a drunken advertising man?' Jack, for one, thought they would, and he was later to be proved right.

Warner accepted it on condition that the film had a happy ending. It didn't. The studio boss was furious, but Warner was in Paris when he found out – by which time it was too late. When the picture was shown before its first audiences, he realized that Lemmon had been right. The happy ending was only for the people who made the picture, not for the audiences – unless they counted the satisfaction they received from seeing a pretty superb picture.

Time magazine had reservations about the film. 'What is missing is a fundamental attempt to understand the social, emotional and spiritual nature of alcoholism. What is wrong is the attempt to be entertaining at all times, even though sometimes the story could be deepened and strengthened by a thoughtful pause.' But for Jack the review had nothing but praise. 'Lemmon's portrayal is easily the most intelligent, intense and complex performance so far accomplished by an actor who started out as a light comedian but apparently can do darn near anything he pleases in front of a camera and most of the time do it better than any American cinema actor of his generation.'

The picture was undoubtedly Jack's best movie to date, and both he and Lee Remick were nominated for Oscars. Once again, however, Jack was the bridesmaid and not the bride. The winner of the Best Actor award was Gregory Peck for his role as the caring lawyer in *To Kill a Mockingbird*. The straw polls that Hollywood conducts each March before the Academy award ceremonies indicated there would be a neck-and-neck struggle between the two actors. A lot of money was on Jack. Greg Peck himself was not sure that Lemmon wouldn't pip him to the post. 'I had seen *Days of Wine and Roses* and thought Jack was superb,' he told me.

It was Sophia Loren who broke the suspense by announcing that Peck had won. As he moved out to the gangway to collect his award, Greg touched Jack lightly on the shoulder. Veronique Peck, who witnessed her husband's gesture, said it seemed to indicate the affection one leading actor had for another. He may not have won the award, but there was the satisfaction of having done that superb job that Peck mentioned. 'I loved *Wine and Roses*,' Jack was to say, but the emotion drained him, just as much as working on the Broadway stage had done. And he hadn't yet got over the travelling to and from the Santa Monica hospital where his father had been treated for the illness that consumed him.

It was precisely the emotion of it all that pervaded Jack's interpretation. Was it just a clown showing he was capable of pathos as part of his craft? Or was there something deeper?

Jack, like his mother, had had a few brushes with the bottle himself, although he wouldn't have qualified for AA membership. Now, he would joke that it was the film that actually drove him *to* drink. Making the movie might reasonably be thought of as the equivalent of taking a series of anti-drink hypnosis sessions, and that after all that brainwashing Jack would as soon drink poison as another martini. But it didn't work that way. Even while making the picture he would still have a drink before dinner and a couple of glasses of wine with his meal.

Drinking provided him with one of his greatest lines of patter, resurrecting a thesis he had written at Harvard about the amount of good liquor displaced by olives. Sitting in a New York bar, he would order his second martini of the evening and very gently, very kindly instruct the waitress on how he wanted his cocktail served. 'Dear, tell the bartender not to put in that olive. An olive replaces from six to eight per cent of the alcohol. At the end of the year, I have paid for a lot of gin, but what I have gotten is olives.'

Other people might have been thought strange, but not Jack. Which, of course, was part of the Lemmon success. He could convince a waitress that he was deadly serious, but was worth a laugh at the same time. That was precisely the effect he had on people who saw *Days of Wine and Roses*.

Hundreds of people wrote to Jack saying that their drinking problems were solved by seeing the film. Others were not cured, but asked for advice. Several wrote more personal letters – telling Jack how he could cure his drink problem if he really joined Alcoholics Anonymous. Some actors would have just laughed, or rudely scorned the advice. Jack sent back carefully considered letters, gratefully accepting the advice which he knew was well-meaning, but explaining that he had been just playing a part.

Some people might have thought it a good idea if he did a *Days of Wine and Roses*-type story on the effect of tobacco. He was a chain-smoker – his excuse was that he needed to burn up his surplus energy – who went through several packets of cigarettes each day. But he knew that wasn't clever, and replaced them with cigars, though he still chain-smokes. They are much longer and much more expensive. But he doesn't think he is inhaling as much nicotine. 'Friends say it's because I never stop talking long enough to smoke them – yap, yap, yap, that's Lemmon.'

But now he was going to be brought under control. In July 1962 he and Felicia starred in an episode of the TV drama series, *The Defenders*. Then he and Shirley MacLaine went off to Romania as part of an American cultural exchange programme. When he came back, he took Christopher on a fishing trip. Very soon afterwards, he was off again – to Paris to make a new film, which before long would mean a whole new life. Jack Uhler Lemmon and Felicia Farr had at last come to an arrangement.

6

The War Between Men and Women

For the moment, few people knew that Jack and Felicia were planning anything special. Jack was in Paris to make a new Billy Wilder film. This was his version of *Irma La Douce*, originally a successful musical, an intimate experience and well suited to small theatres, but which Wilder believed could transfer to the big screen as a comedy. He couldn't see Jack in a musical but he knew this story about the *gendarme* who falls for the Parisian prostitute with the proverbial heart of gold, and who becomes her pimp, was ideal casting for his friend. He also knew that Jack couldn't play it like a young Maurice Chevalier, but as a Californian juvenile who somehow found himself in Paris. Most of the interest in the film centred around Jack's original co-star, the lovely lady of the Paris streets, who was to be Elizabeth Taylor. But before long the role was firmly in the hands, and everything else, of Shirley MacLaine.

Felicia too was in Paris, but then she always was with Jack when he was working on a film so there was no reason to imagine anything out of the ordinary was going on. Then Jack announced to his friends that he and Felicia were to get married. In fact, the wedding would take place in a few days' time, on 15 August 1962, and in that city. It was to be organized with all the efficiency of a Hollywood film – and with all the things going wrong which could be expected with Jack Lemmon being involved. There was a bridegroom, and a bride, and she had chosen her matron of honour, Billy Wilder's wife Audrey. The problems arose with the selection of Jack's best man. It was more than just a job to be done at a wedding ceremony. It was a statement of whom Jack regarded as his best, his closest friend.

It can present difficulties to anyone. To Jack it took on the dimensions of a crisis. He was risking upsetting the friend he didn't choose – and what was more, he couldn't choose. His solution was simple. He appointed two best men, Billy Wilder and Richard Quine. The story that both best men tell could form part of a comedy film starring a rejuvenated Jack Lemmon.

Billy Wilder had to rehearse Jack for the civil ceremony, which was to be performed by the Mayor of Paris himself. 'The incredible thing', he told me, 'is this man who can remember pages and pages of dialogue and never, never fluffs a line, had to be coached to remember one word in French.' Wilder told Jack that when the Mayor says in French, 'Do you Jack Uhler Lemmon take this woman Felicia Farr to be your wife?' he had to say just one word, '*Oui*'. It was simple enough, but Wilder said he would poke Jack in the ribs with his elbow at the critical moment, just to be sure.

Richard Quine was also in Paris, directing *Paris When It Sizzles*. Since there were a number of other professional movie people around, he made sure nothing would go wrong. Quine planned to stage-manage Felicia's entrance with all the precision of the last American entry into France, the Normandy landings. Needless to say, he had a cast of extras all lined up to make sure that the wheels were sufficiently well oiled – led by Shirley MacLaine and Audrey Hepburn, who was starring in Quine's film. He arranged his own movie's shooting schedule so that they would be filming at the Elysées Park Hotel, the very place where Felicia was staying. While his team operated downstairs, Felicia was getting dressed upstairs. Quine and Wilder had got together, pooling their two movies' resources to film the historic moment when Jack finally made an honest woman of Felicia.

Audrey Wilder was helping to get her ready as Quine shot a necessary scene – but one that was organized to cover both functions – with Audrey Hepburn going up and down in the prestigious hotel's open-cage lift. 'We had arranged things so that when Felicia came down in the elevator, we would photograph her, and that we'd do it again going through the lobby on the way to the wedding,' Quine explained. The crew had gladioli ready to make into a tunnel of flowers for the future Mrs Jack Lemmon to walk through. 'But that bloody elevator must have gone up and down ten times with Audrey Hepburn in it,' Quine told me. 'She was to report to us when the bride was ready. But we never knew. We couldn't give her a walkie-talkie or anything, because that would give the game away. So the elevator went up with Audrey Hepburn in it and came down with Audrey Hepburn in it. And she'd say, "It's going to be another ten minutes." So we'd wait ten minutes. And then the elevator buzzer would ring and we would put Audrey back in the elevator and send her back again – only for it to stop on the wrong floor. Finally, she came down again and said, "Next time. Give it three minutes. When the buzzer rings, she'll be ready." She went up again and this time down came Felicia and Audrey Wilder and Audrey Hepburn, all in the same elevator.'

At last, it seemed all was well. Except . . . 'It was one of the worst directing jobs in my life,' Quine recalled, almost blushing as he told me what happened next. 'I forgot to tell Audrey that Wilder was photographing it all and wanted to see Felicia.' As the lift came down, Audrey Wilder was fixing something on Felicia's hair and standing right in front of her – and no one could see Felicia. When they looked at the film later there was just a glimpse of her going through the gladioli.

That problem out of the way, there was room for more. Such as the white Rolls-Royce which Quine was using in his film and which he now made available for the bigger production of the Lemmon–Farr marriage. His property department arranged to decorate it suitably – with the biggest catering-size cans he could get hold of. The ceremony was another matter. At the critical moment Wilder poked Jack in the ribs. No response. 'What's that word?' asked the bridegroom. It was the only line Jack ever had trouble with. On the way back to the Hotel George V where the reception was being held, the Rolls with its tin cans clattered and rumbled its way along the cobbled roads, much to the astonishment of the poor Parisians. Only later on did Quine discover that tying tin cans to a wedding car is *not* a French custom.

But the reception went ahead without incident in a suite specially decorated for the occasion by Quine and his art department – with lemon trees on one side and olive branches on the other. The director-cum-decorator knew what few others did – that Felicia's real name was Olive. 'Cost of filming that day, I am afraid, was down to Paramount' – the studio which was making *Paris When It Sizzles*.

Jack and Felicia were at the start of what everyone was again calling Hollywood's happiest marriage – made none the less happy by the number of times the pair still shouted and made up. True to form, Jack fell in the Seine shortly after the wedding – he was supposed to do it in the film, but this time it was accidental – and swallowed enough of the foul water to have a serious stomach upset. It wasn't an ideal way of spending a honeymoon.

From the moment of the wedding on, Jack's *Irma La Douce* could have been either a French farce or *Macbeth*. Whatever Wilder wanted of him, Wilder could have. He was as happy as the young ensign who discovered he still had the right flag to fly. This time he was signalling to everyone in sight that he had never been happier. He joked with the *Irma* crew, he played his songs, he signed autographs. If there were visitors to a set, he happily posed for photographs for them. All that Jack always did, but this time he did it with extra enthusiasm. 'Jack has to be liked by everybody,' said Felicia at the time. 'Even the associate producer's second secretary.'

At the end of a day's shooting he held open house in his dressing-room, dispensing drinks like a soda jerk in a Los Angeles drugstore. Everyone who walked in had a personal welcome – whether they were old friends, casual acquaintances or simply the kind of people who like mingling with film stars and somehow or other break through the various security barriers installed for the occasion. Everybody was greeted by name, if he knew it. When he didn't, it was a warm hello to 'old buddy', 'dear boy', or just 'kid' or 'baby'.

Jack would have loved *Irma La Douce* even if it had been a flop, because of the romantic associations the film would always have for him. Before starting work on *Irma* Jack did what he always did whenever he first went on to a film set or a live stage. He shouted:

An early publicity shot of Columbia's new star, Jack Lemmon.

Lemmon with Judy Holliday in his first film. *It Should Happen To You* made
him an international star overnight.

With Marge and Gower Champion and Betty Grable in *Three For The Show*,
Lemmon's first musical.

On location in Hawaii for *Mister Roberts*. Jack relaxing with (*from left*) James Cagney (the captain) William Powell (the doctor), Henry Fonda (the title role) and Ward Bond (the petty officer).

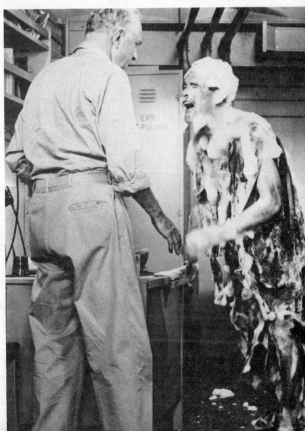

Lemmon as Ensign Pulver in the famous "bubbles" scene in *Mister Roberts*.

Starring with the beautiful Rita Hayworth in *Fire Down Below*.

Lemmon the musician. Behind the scenes, Jack plays the background score he composed for *Fire Down Below*.

Lemmon with Tony Curtis (*left*) disguised as girl musicians in Billy Wilder's classic comedy, *Some Like It Hot*.

Another scene from *Some Like It Hot*, with Marilyn Monroe on the beach at Miami.

Kim Novak and Jack Lemmon – the divorced couple who go to court simply to find out what's been missing between them in *Phffft*.

Lemmon in his bachelor pad at Bel Air,
and right, checking his star-gazing
equipment on the terrace.

Jack with Shirley MacLaine in
Billy Wilder's film *The Apartment*.

With producer-director Billy Wilder –
discussing one of Jack's first serious roles
in *The Apartment*.

Lemmon's mobile face, contorted into that of the gendarme playing the pimp in *Irma La Douce*.

In Paris for *Irma La Douce* with his bride-to-be Felicia Farr and with Billy Wilder. Jack hides behind his bushy eyebrows and false beard.

Hollywood's most famous sparring partners – united at last. With director Richard Quine (who shared the job of best man with Billy Wilder), the organizer of the wedding ceremony, looking on.

Two contrasting scenes from *Days of Wine and Roses*, one of Jack's finest films. Both with his co-star Lee Remick.

There was little odd about Jack's relationship with his close friend Walter Matthau. The film was, however, called *The Odd Couple*.

Lemmon enjoying a lecture session at London's National Film Theatre.

The Lemmons with their daughter Courtney at Heathrow Airport, London.

In *The War Between Men and Women*, Jack is sandwiched between his new wife, Barbara Harris, and her first husband Jason Robards Jr.

Giving advice to his friend and star Walter Matthau while making *Kotch* in 1971. It was Lemmon's first attempt at directing.

A study in anguish from *Save the Tiger*. It won Jack his second Oscar.

With co-star Lee Remick, who played Jack's ex-wife in *Tribute*.

Lemmon could use some of his own real-life emotional experience in facing his son (Robby Benson) in *Tribute*.

More agony in the interpretation of the father searching for his murdered son in *Missing*. With Sissy Spacek as his daughter-in-law.

A moment of relaxation while making *Tribute* in 1980.

'magic time!' It wasn't merely superstition, although it took on the proportions of that. It was also a plain declaration of fact. He was enjoying every moment of his work and others would, too.

He made *The Apartment* much funnier than Wilder had intended; now the same thing happened with *Irma La Douce*. This time Wilder promised himself, 'I'm not going to let him do all those marvellous tricks. But I'm helpless. Jack's talent seduced me. I'm too weak to resist.'

Jack did his research the way he always did. This time, however, it was more pleasant than it had been before *Days of Wine and Roses*. He visited French brothels – with Shirley MacLaine in tow for safety. For hours they talked to the ladies of that particular night and to the madame. The women would excuse themselves every few minutes to deal with clients upstairs. 'They were very proud of their fast turnover,' he said of his interrupted conversations. Then he admitted, 'Our eyes were as big as saucers.'

Time magazine loved the reunion of Wilder's stars from *The Apartment* in 1963: '*Irma* bubbles and struts through every Technicolor foot. Shirley MacLaine is an adorable golliwog in green lingerie and inky wig. Her flamboyant self-assurance is the perfect foil for the bumbling Lemmon. With a face that can twinkle like a terrier's or crumple into bloodhoundish gloom at the first unkind word, Jack makes the most – once he's fired as a cop – of being Shirley's *mec*, the only pimp in Paris with the principles of an eagle scout.'

If only the momentum could have been maintained – but that success was followed by a couple of career mistakes. The first was called *Under the Yum Yum Tree*, in which he played the lecherous landlord of two college students experiencing what in those days was called a trial marriage. It was sold as a sex farce and Jack gave the impression that he wanted to hide his face. It is generally accepted as the worst movie of his career – though the picture was not a failure at the box office and the feeling was that if he could do so well with such a dreadful movie, then he must be a very great star indeed.

His next picture was *Good Neighbor Sam*. This time he was involved in the post-marital adventures of the divorcee next door. Once again, it was being sold as a sex comedy. When he saw the script, he said, 'This is just a piece of smut,' and twice ordered it to be rewritten. But his problems were not over. He then fought with Columbia's advertising and publicity departments, who started to put out posters proclaiming: 'It's that Yum Yum Man Again'. Lemmon later admitted that he didn't check the synopses properly before he and his old studio came to a deal. He had the contract with Columbia to make a picture a year and he was merely fulfilling his obligations in a way that was totally contrary to his usual approach to his work.

At the time, however, he tried to prove that there were a lot of plus factors in the role of Sam. 'The guy had a lot of faults, thank God. Because if there's anything I can't stand it's a faultless character.' And he went on, 'The better the writing is, the more elusive the character is. Just as it is with human beings. We're all chameleons.' Perhaps it would be kind to say that Jack found the *Good Neighbor Sam* character very easily indeed. But he didn't. He was no more happy with the lack of depth of the man next door than were most audiences, who still paid willingly for the opportunity to see him.

What really got his friends worried was that he had now appeared in three sex films in a row. He was having to make excuses for them, a state of affairs totally foreign to Jack Lemmon so far. The weakest excuse, he freely admitted, was that *Yum Yum Tree* had been contracted with Columbia a full three years before it was made, a time when his own tastes, to say nothing of those of his audiences, were perhaps a little less sophisticated. It did not help matters that his next film was called *How to Murder Your Wife*. The movie was made by a division of Jalem Productions in conjunction with United Artists. They called the new company, set up to offload the expenses, Murder Inc. As he told Louella Parsons, 'I think if *Days of Wine and Roses* had come between *Irma* and *Yum Yum*, I wouldn't have gotten the criticism I did. We've all been up in arms lately about a breach of taste in films. I never know quite how to talk about this whole area of sex and films because it involves so many other people. I should really duck it, but I don't. I'll tell you honestly I don't think there's anything offensive in *How to Murder Your Wife*. If there is, I give up. It's no more offensive than the great comedies of the past, like the sophisticated ones of the Lubitsch era which everybody misses. It's not a sex comedy. It's a comedy about the battle of the sexes.'

Felicia summed up a lot that could be said about the attitude of people who thought they were being kind to Jack by saying how good he was. 'You can't trust anybody,' she said. 'People say things they don't mean. I am the cynic in the family. I'm the heavy. All day long, I walk around saying, "Bah, humbug!"'

Jack was more understanding. But it helped to know that he wasn't the only one to make a mistake. When Billy Wilder flopped with *Kiss Me Stupid* – a Dean Martin film featuring hitherto undiscovered Gershwin music (listening to it, one understood why it had been undiscovered) which the director told me he didn't care to remember – Jack was full of understanding for his old friend. 'He tried a sex satire and missed. The more talent you have the more capable you are of missing . . . Billy Wilder missed. He's entitled.'

It was Jack's attitude to what other people would regard as failure that Wilder says is one of his most endearing qualities. 'I've been with him through very good pictures, through successes and through failures, but Jack's attitude never changes.' And he went on, 'When you have had a series of flops, what happens in this town is very perceptible, if you are sensitive. The policeman at the entrance to the gate is smiling not quite so cheerily as when you had a succession of hits. Somehow you don't get the table you want at a restaurant. You discover you have not been asked to be a pallbearer at someone important's funeral. You are not quite in demand as you were. The phone calls are a little bit rarer. People tend to divert their attention to those who are successful at the moment. Not so with Jack. After a string of flops, he'll say, "When do we do the next one?" Or, without seeing a script, "Have you got anything for me? If you have, when do we go?" It is that most marvellous vote of confidence you get from him that I love him for so very much.'

Jack was asked if he was one of those clowns who dream of playing Hamlet. No side with him there. No protestations that he was above all that. He said that he would have loved to – 'but I haven't got the equipment. Maybe when I'm eighty years old, I'll

89

put on youth make-up.' That was why he was toying with what he agreed was a patently ridiculous idea – trying to improve the quality of television by playing Iago on the small screen.

At the same time there were disappointments in his personal life. He wasn't really seeing enough of Christopher to please him – he would have enjoyed having the child living under his roof, but Cynthia had custody. And he had just lost a very good friend. Ernie Kovacs, who at one time had looked as if he was all set to be a permanent Lemmon partner, had died – an event which Jack said made him stop and think.

But in 1963 he was named Star of the Year by the United Theatre Owners of the Heart of America – a just award to the man who was more and more proving himself to be one of their principal meal tickets, some eight years after he had come out to Hollywood for the first time. His success meant money in the bank. Plainly his bachelor pad at the top of Bel Air was no longer suitable for a newly married couple, and Felicia was so decorative he did not want to shut her away from view. The couple bought a French provincial home in Tower Road, Beverly Hills, near Fred Astaire's house.

Life magazine asked the question: 'Does everyone here like Jack Lemmon?' and came to the conclusion that everybody really did. He was liked enough by the big studios to be worth a million dollars every time he signed a new contract.

He wasn't always liked by the husbands of beautiful women. There was, for instance, the case of Virna Lisi and her husband. Signora Lisi made other women's curves look like straight lines. She was an Italian actress who had the power to turn strong men to jelly, and she played the victim in *How to Murder Your Wife*.

It seemed more likely that Virna's husband wanted to murder Jack, especially when he casually walked into the voluptuous lady's dressing-room and found her standing in front of a mirror totally naked. Her husband was sitting on the couch and didn't take Jack's familiarity at all kindly. 'What he didn't realize was that all the dressing-rooms looked alike,' Quine, again the director, told me, 'and Jack thought he was walking into his own.' Later, the Lisis and the Lemmons became firm friends.

But it was no thanks to the film. Jack played a cartoonist who uses his drawings to ease his frustration at not being able to get rid of his wife. He plans on paper ways he would like to use to kill her, although actually doing it is the last thing on his mind. 'It's a flashy, wonderful part,' he told Louella Parsons, who had heard a few stories about marvellous films before then. 'If I were offered it tomorrow, I'd do it all over again. It's so glib, sophisticated and well written. I just hope it doesn't fly right by the audience.'

On the whole it did. The movie, said the *Sunday Telegraph*, 'is a sort of recruiting film for the Playboy Clubs, a facetious harangue on the pleasures of bachelordom for fat old men who are frightened of girls but like thinking about them.'

But Jack still had the comfort of knowing that, as far as the audiences were concerned, he was still Mr Perfect. He had just been named the number-one male box-office attraction for 1964, second only to Doris Day in all-round popularity. Rock Hudson, John Wayne and Cary Grant all appeared in the same list, trailing behind Jack.

And then he had a reunion with Tony Curtis. The film was *The Great Race* which Jalem, Jack's own company, made in conjunction with Warner Brothers in 1965. Though it was no *Some Like It Hot*, it cost a great deal more. It was based on a real turn-of-the-century car race and seemed, on the new wide screen, like Warners' answer to *Around the World in Eighty Days*. There were bar-room brawls in the Wild West, gold-rushes in Alaska, a trip to Ruritania à la *Prisoner of Zenda* and all the time Tony Curtis was the hero in a white suit and Jack, Professor Fate, the villain in black – complete with twirly moustache that no one could possibly believe wasn't stuck to his upper lip with glue.

Tony Curtis played the Great Leslie, but it was Fate most people noticed. 'Fate is a nut,' Jack said, 'a psychotic, the overt cartoon image of the arch-villain. Picture the worst Shakespearean actor you've ever seen, really bad, but with more confidence than Olivier.' All the players seemed to have had a great time hamming it up like a Victorian melodrama – among them beautiful Natalie Wood, playing a suffragette reporter who not only had mud pies thrust into her face but got herself involved in a series of escapades no decent feminist would care to admit to. Natalie was exceedingly impressed with Jack. She told me shortly before her death: 'He was wonderful in that film. I have never seen anyone able to go in so many different directions, identifying every character he plays so perfectly and finely.'

There was plenty to laugh at – and cheer, particularly when the devilish Professor strikes a match on his front teeth. It wasn't exactly sophisticated, although Curtis was heard to mutter that Jack thought he was a lot funnier than he actually was. He even suggested to a reporter that Jack was 'really rather corny, which is very appealing'. It's a cliché to talk about how hard it is to play comedy, but Jack has always been the embodiment of it. On *The Great Race*, as in all the others, he worked for his laughs as though he were digging a hole in the road. If, after a succession of takes, he was finally satisfied with his work, and it looked as though it had all happened naturally, then there was a good chance audiences would laugh too.

Actually Jack's practical jokes on the set were a lot funnier than Curtis allowed. *The Great Race* happened at the time when Lemmon's preoccupation with pool was rivalling that with his piano. Jack had indicated it would be nice to have a pool table on the set and Bill Orr happily obliged. 'It was a pleasure to do so,' Orr told me. 'Jack never made any demands. We never had any fuss from him about requirements for his own dressing-room or anything like that.'

What had begun as a mere diversion on the set of *The Notorious Landlady* was fast becoming an essential part of the Lemmon day. He and his two cohorts on the *Landlady* film, Fred Astaire and Dick Quine, had a regular midweek game. Now a giant-sized pool table, as heavy a bit of equipment as anything normally used in a film studio, was moved by grips from one location to the next. They used heavy-duty fork-lift trucks. It was Jack's idea to brighten up the day by bringing his personal dentist, Sheffield, to join in the regular studio game. What he didn't tell his fellow player, Peter Falk, was that 'Dr Sheffield' was a professional pool player by the name of Jimmy Carras, who won hands down every time he picked up his cue. 'If you fill teeth like you play pool,' Falk told the guest, 'you're the greatest dentist in the world.' Jack enjoyed that.

Blake Edwards was no Billy Wilder but his direction was deft, and the race, from New York to Paris, was sufficiently good fun for the film to be one of America's entries at the Fourth Moscow International Film Festival. The others were *To Kill a Mockingbird*, Henry Fonda's *The Best Man* and *Lilies of the Field*, with Sidney Poitier.

The Great Race won a silver prize. 'With all those message films being shown,' Jack told the *New York Times*, 'we brought in this wild idiot farce, and some very interesting things happened.' The most interesting of all was that the 2,500-strong Russian audience – helped by having the dialogue dubbed in their own language – loved it. They had gone through the other American entries, all important films which either had messages or were intended to make people think. 'Then we showed *The Great Race* – $11 million-worth of sheer fluff. They let out a guffaw at the beginning of the picture and then never stopped laughing for three hours.'

The film scored, too, in that it was totally devoid of anything that could be recognized as political propaganda. Jack himself couldn't understand why a 'cultural swap' like that wasn't also held in Hollywood. 'Nothing is solved by lack of communication,' he said, something which he found out when he and his party landed in Russia for the first time. There had been an unexpected storm over Moscow itself and their plane was diverted to another airport – where no one knew who they were or why they were there. Finally, a series of Russian-language forms were thrust at them – which no one was able to read, let alone sign. 'Things were at an impasse for four steaming hours,' Jack later reported. 'First we had to stand in one queue and then another and then someone who spoke French had the bright idea of giving us French forms to fill out, which we did and they finally allowed us to leave.'

He left the film festival a lot happier than when he arrived, and on his return to Hollywood signed a new deal with Columbia – again on behalf of Jalem Productions. The company would make six films for Columbia, in four of which Jack would star himself. Jack would have 'creative control' of this output. That in itself wasn't new. He had been doing as much as he could since *Days of Wine and Roses*, but it was a sense of authority confirmed. And, as he put it, a chance of falling on his own fanny. 'You don't stay awake nights blaming the boss,' he said, 'because you are the boss.' He liked the idea of going to an office when he wasn't standing in front of the lights. He enjoyed working with the directors and writers. 'That's great,' he said. 'I want to be immersed until just before shooting, when Lemmon the actor takes over. Then I want to delegate the responsibility to other people so that I'm not at all – hopefully not one inch – detracting from the performance I should give.'

Jack had arrived back in Beverly Hills in time for a new arrival in the family. On 7 January 1966 Felicia gave birth to her second daughter, and their first child together. They called her Courtney. Fatherhood to Jack is the ideal state. He is passionate about being an actor, but ever since he first handled a baby of his own, he knew no joy like it.

He was still enjoying that role with Christopher, and their regular fishing trips were some of Jack's happiest days. Chris was ten now, and his father was beginning to wonder whether there mightn't be some like-father-like-son acting talent in him. On one outing the child vanished, and Jack eventually found him on the beach with a pile of cocktail frankfurters, shouting out: 'Get your ice-cold lemonade, twenty-five cents a glass!' Now that is the kind of story any father likes telling about his children; but with Jack it had a purpose. 'That's when I realized that it was just what I'm doing all the time. There was nobody on the beach for miles in any direction, except Chris. But I am making believe, just like a kid, and I'm happy as a kid, too.'

When Chris played in a Little League baseball team, Jack had to abandon his business meetings to be sure of being there on time. 'The team has so far won one out of thirteen,' he said explaining his need to get away for the event. 'Chris has had two hits. Well, not hits, exactly – he's hit the ball two times. I keep telling the coach, he's near-sighted. For-get it.'

It was Jack's favourite way of talking about his favourite subjects. A word divided into distinct syllables conveyed a sense of affection or pleasure. When he took over an old office vacated by Elvis Presley, he contemplated the used guitar strings likely to be lying on the floor, and said, 'Ter-rif-ic.'

Jack's mother had now moved to Los Angeles to be near him and had transferred all her allegiances from the Ritz-Carlton in Boston to the bar of the Bell Air Hotel. She got on well with Felicia, although she may have been puzzled as to whether Jack was, for the fights continued. 'I think it's very healthy,' said Jack. Felicia was content to agree that their quarrels were about 'everything and nothing'.

There were still occasions when she threatened to leave him. 'I frighten him,' she said once, 'by telling him he can have *everything* – the children, the house, the responsibility of everything. Because that's what the women are all left with – leaky plumbing, incompetent help, and no husband to share the misery with.' When she did storm out, it was only to work out how she was going to get back into the house again. She'd get into her car and drive around the block. Then perhaps she would go to a movie. 'He's cottoned on to that. Now he says when I return, "What picture did you see?"'

There were occasions when she very successfully made her husband the butt of her practical jokes – like the time the phone rang. A schoolgirl was on the end of the line, apologizing profusely, asking if Mr Lemmon – whose number she just happened to get hold of – could get her a job on the stage. Rightly, she judged that the always polite and considerate Jack Lemmon wouldn't just palm her off or give her a rude answer. But he felt he had to tell the young lady the truth. 'You see,' he said, 'it's very, very difficult.' Finally, the polite side of his nature beginning to fray at the edges, he had to say there was no chance of his being able to help the girl. She poured buckets of tears into the mouthpiece. 'Listen,' he said, 'there are professionals without work – why should I try to get a job for you, whom I don't even know. I wouldn't have the nerve to ask for a job for my own wife.'

'Not even for your wife?' questioned the sobbing voice.

'No,' he said. 'Not even if she were the best actress for a part.'

'Well,' replied the voice at the other end, suddenly more mature, and more familiar. 'You're a dirty b— '

Felicia then put down the phone in her bedroom and stormed down the stairs to berate her husband for his lack of consideration. And then she locked herself in a closet, while Jack almost put his hand through the door for the second time. 'You have to really care very, very deeply about someone to let her upset you so much,' he said in explanation.

Felicia was continuing to make the occasional film herself – although Jack said that she really didn't work enough. She would claim that she didn't have the push to make it big in films, and hadn't done anything since an appearance in that Billy Wilder flop *Kiss Me Stupid*. But she observed Jack and his work and suffered with him. As she said, 'He's always convinced he doesn't know the character. When he starts a picture the first weeks are hell. Everything's wrong. He talks about it all the time.'

Now, with the new Columbia contract, he was talking about another picture for Billy Wilder. The old firm was going back into business again – and this time with a new starring partner, Walter Matthau.

7
The Odd Couple

Walter Matthau soon found out that it was impossible not to like Jack Lemmon. As Sidney Poitier said: 'You won't find anything wrong with him. But if you do, for heaven's sake let the rest of us know about it.'

The picture Wilder had in mind for the two of them in the latest Jalem production was *The Fortune Cookie* – a title that wasn't expected to mean anything in Britain where it would be called *Meet Whiplash Willie*. Wilder would produce as well as direct and write the screenplay, yet again with I. A. L. Diamond.

Jack and Walter had known of each other's work, of course, but until Wilder introduced them on the set of *The Fortune Cookie* they had never actually met. Once the film was completed, Matthau was saying that Lemmon was his best friend. Wilder told me they were like brothers. And Jack described him when we met as 'my wife'. But unlike Jack's real wife, Jack and Walter never quarrelled. 'We each know what the other's next move is going to be,' he said, 'We think for each other. It's uncanny.'

Their film was the story of a sharp lawyer who decides to sue for $1 million compensation when his client, a television cameraman, is slightly injured covering a football game. The ball hits his head. He is only slightly injured, but the lawyer decides that there is enough of a molehill for him to construct a mountain. Jack played the client – and spent most of his time on screen trussed up and tied to a wheelchair. Walter was the lawyer, Whiplash Willie.

It was a slight story. The client was always the frustrated one, sitting helplessly in his chair while the lawyer looked up loopholes in the law and created sufficient shenanigans to get himself instantly disbarred. Without the masterly performance demanded for the lawyer's role, the film would have shrunk without trace. Jack could have done it himself and achieved all the success of Professor Fate and the hapless proprietor of *The Apartment*, but he wanted Walter to have it.

'There you have something else about Jack,' said Billy Wilder. 'The man's incredible generosity. Any other actor in Jack's position would immediately look for the best part for himself, but no. Jack thought Walter could do with it.' He also knew that Matthau could do well with it, which isn't necessarily the same thing. Walter couldn't understand Jack's generosity either. After all, he wasn't just the star of the film, he was the head of the production company making it, for God's sake. Jack simply told him it was about time he started making an honest living, too.

Matthau had been a successful Broadway actor, starring in some twenty-eight plays, whom very few people outside of the New York theatre milieu had ever heard of. He went to Hollywood in early middle age in search of a chance of stardom, and when he did get a role, it was usually small, as in the Dean Martin–Lana Turner movie *Who's Got the Action*, in which he also played a less than savoury character. In Elvis Presley's *King Creole* he was a crook. In *Charade* and *Mirage* he was a useful supporting actor. In both these films he was something of a mystery man – which described his position in Hollywood perfectly. He did what he had to do well, but he hadn't had the opportunity to be a big star. He played a sheriff in *Lonely Are the Brave*, another small part, but an exceptional one. But he still wasn't a star. When an opportunity *had* presented itself – to play opposite Marilyn Monroe in *The Seven Year Itch* in the part of the deserted husband who suddenly discovers the girl upstairs –the producer Charles K. Feldman thought he needed someone better known. He chose Tom Ewell, who wasn't well known at all, but did the job. Jack knew all that and happily gave Walter the part of Whiplash Willie – without realizing that his fellow actor was about to come down with a massive heart attack.

Matthau told me the attack made him think anew of his life.

'Until you have a heart attack – why it happened no one knew, I hadn't had a heart condition – you feel you're suddenly mortal. You can't say, "Wait a minute, I can't die yet. I'm still in the middle of the season." You *can* die.' He was going to give up the gambling that had already lost him a large rather than a small fortune, and he was going to take his work much more easily. In *The Fortune Cookie* it looked natural, and Walter came out the winner.

Billy Wilder says that the picture wasn't a great success. But it was enough. The two men in the film were supposed to be brothers-in-law – an added dimension to the story that they both handled beautifully. In no small way they were helped, too, by Billy Wilder's writing. Despite Wilder's assertion to me that he has always been receptive to ideas, Jack denied that he would ever change a word of his dialogue – in scripts that the producer-director-writer sometimes wrote out actually on the set, just before the scenes were about to be shot. 'You don't ad lib Wilder,' said Jack, 'just as you don't ad lib Shakespeare. . . . There is no question of *interpreting* the author, wondering what he might mean. Billy knows precisely because he *is* the author.'

The Fortune Cookie was another opportunity for the two men, director and star, to consolidate their mutual affection and admiration. Jack particularly liked Billy's attention to detail. He said he noticed a speck of dust on a prop, 'a flicker of an eyelid that isn't right. I've never known anyone so alert. Billy never misses a trick.'

It was that implicit trust in Wilder that persuaded Jack to welcome Walter Matthau so warmly – and undoubtedly why Matthau's performance in *The Fortune Cookie* was so right. Jack allowed Walter to get most of the applause as well as the best lines, very much at his own expense. *Time* summed up what a lot of others felt: 'Director Billy Wilder has taken the rash risk in this film of spiking his big gun. In *Cookie*, he keeps Jack Lemmon, a funnyman-in-motion who lacks the instincts of a sit-down comedian, sitting in a wheelchair that makes him seem foolish but never funny. With Lemmon immobilized, only a miracle could save the show from being as sedative as Wilder's last picture *Kiss Me Stupid*. Fortunately something like a miracle is at hand : Walter Matthau.'

Walter won an Academy Award, Jack's undying love and friendship, and the certainty that the two of them were on the verge of what before long would be a sort of Laurel and Hardy team who every now and again came together but between times did their own things on their own. 'They kind of clicked,' Billy Wilder told me. 'They were inseparable from the very first day.' They had their very own language early on, too – using phrases the other understood better than anyone else. Walter wasn't happy to call his friend 'Jack' the same as everyone else. To him, he was Uhler. After all those years, Jack's middle name was taken out and given an airing. Socially, too, they had much in common – a sympathy with the Democratic party, a love of good citizenship, and Carol Matthau and Felicia completed the circle.

Jack was very hot playing his good citizen role. At about the time he was making *The Fortune Cookie*, doing the location shots at the Cleveland Browns' stadium, Jack saw a hit-and-run driver, gave chase and then provided the local police with all the necessary information. The following week he was subpoenaed to testify in court. He found it harder than making a picture.

When his work on *The Fortune Cookie* was over, he started on a new picture for Jalem, the first in which he didn't star. *Cool Hand Luke*, a chain-gang story, was not up his own street, so he awarded the role to Paul Newman. It wasn't easy to pass a leading role to another player without doing anything himself on the screen – much harder than sitting down while Matthau played in *Fortune Cookie*. At least in that, he was still taking direction and looking into the lens of a camera the right way. In *Cool Hand Luke*, he was simply – an understatement which he was to discover wasn't simple at all – an executive.

As one of his colleagues noted at the time: 'Jack is a reluctant tycoon. The tycoon image doesn't quite fit. He's just too disorganized, too human to fit that description.' So disorganized that when Felicia bought him a radiophone for his car as a birthday present, he said that it wasn't him and he wouldn't want to use it, ever. He changed his mind when he had three punctures in his car on three successive days, and needed the phone to call out a garage. However, the phone didn't merely give him a chance to rid himself of a problem, it gave him a new one. He kept forgetting to 'sign off' – which meant that he was charged with calls that lasted twenty-four hours each. Another time, he left the phone off the hook for a complete weekend. It not only brought a hefty bill, it also meant that the car battery was flat.

He regarded his new work as a day-by-day challenge. He explained: 'For an actor, life can get pretty dull between pictures. I'm busy enough. I have no complaints. But between pictures, short as the intervals are, I become impatient. And I don't always like the way scripts are altered, sometimes affecting my roles. But the people responsible for the film, such as a major company, have the right to say what's right. Having my own company, I keep busy and have my autonomy. An additional satisfaction is the feeling of creativity. An actor seldom creates in the true sense. A script is handed to him and he interprets his part. As an independent producer ... I can look at the finished product, whether or not I appear in it as an actor, and enjoy the gratification of having contributed to it in the true creative sense.'

But when *Cool Hand Luke* was finished, he confessed himself nothing less than delighted. 'I hadn't produced it, I hadn't directed it, I wasn't in it,' he said, 'but I got more excitement than I'd ever had from seeing myself on the screen.' But he wasn't in film-making simply because of the business potential. 'I'm a lousy businessman,' he claimed, 'I'm an actor first, an executive second.'

His production company was rapidly becoming very big business, though there were some unexpected problems in setting it up. Word was put out that as Jack was such a nice, decent guy with such nice, decent contacts he would be able to gather all the talent he needed for his pictures at below the market rate, an I-can-get-it-for-you operation involving all his friends. Contrary to rumours, Jack tended to overpay those working for Jalem, and he got top people. Much of his success was due to the creative and executive back-up he established with Gordon Carroll, the man he appointed executive producer. 'I've always thought that creative people in films were underpaid, not overpaid,' he said of the actors he used in his first productions. 'We hear talk of vast pay, but then we only keep about fifteen per cent of it, and anyway, an actor's professional life can be short and out of his control. He can be the victim of whim, of fashion, and he needs to earn the money while he can. It's all really feast-to-famine talk. Last year can be a great year, this year can be a great year, and then a couple of flops and, oh boy, it's zero the year after.' On the barometer of the success of Jack Lemmon at the end of the 1960s there was no sign at all of 'oh boy, it's zero'.

'If an actor uses his head he can make good movies, show profits and turn in credible performances,' he declared. He always admitted he would 'do anything' if he liked a story, and in 1966 he took a chance with a play called *Luv* by Murray Shisgal. It was the story of a man's attempts to prevent a close friend from committing suicide, and the subsequent repercussions of bringing him to stay at home. The play had been a success on Broadway and in London, and Jack worked closely with the British director Clive Donner and screenplay writer Elliott Baker.

Henry Berlin, the character Jack played, was a real challenge. He was a skinny scarecrow of a man who was unkind to virtually everybody, something which was almost impossible for Jack to convey. To achieve the 138-pound figure his character was supposed to have Jack shed 30 pounds. Instead of having his meals in the studio's executive dining-room he could be seen lining up with the lesser mortals on the lot to buy a thirty-cent ham sandwich. He wore ill-fitting suits and hats that looked like Salvation Army rejects, and he immersed himself in *Luv* as though he were convinced it would win him an Oscar.

All in all it was an honourable failure. The British Film Institute's *Monthly Film Bulletin* wrote of it: 'A light but incisive comedy about the patterns and language of love in a Freud-ridden society has become an inept and lethally unamusing film farce.' Nonetheless it was the kind of part Jack would try for again and again. He felt it helped him to lose the predictability of Lemmon movies. Although he protested that he didn't have an image on screen, there was always the famous Jack Lemmon charm, the sort of charm that permeated through the most unattractive characters he portrayed, and which was still very much in evidence off the movie lot.

The ultra-smart dinner at the home of the former Hollywood tycoon William Goetz was a case in point. It was a very smart occasion and Jack, as the current top male box-office success, was a prized guest. The guest of honour was publisher's wife Mrs Gardner Cowles, who was placed next to Jack. The first sign of trouble ahead came when the waiter, beautifully turned out in tails and wearing the requisite white gloves, brought in a salver of red pickled cabbage. Jack, in a continental mood, was eating, not American style with the fork in his right hand, but with a knife and fork together. What exactly happened to the knife, fork and red cabbage that evening isn't clear, but poor Mrs Cowles ended up, Jack later reported, 'like a walking blood clot'. Somehow a large helping of cabbage had made its way on to his fellow guest's exquisite evening dress.

Jack was stunned – if not quite as much as Mrs Cowles. Felicia looked as if she were about to attack him with her fork. There was nothing for him to do but brazen it out. He chinked his glass with a spoon, stood up and said: 'I demand a clean dinner partner.' Lemmon the klutz was saved.

But there was more sadness in Jack's family life. His mother Millie died on 4 September 1967. She was expected at the Lemmon house that day, and Felicia had dressed the baby ready to receive her grandmother. It was going to be the kind of pleasant family day Jack would have loved to have had in his own childhood. As always on these occasions, he drove out to Millie's apartment to pick her up – a smile on his face, a joke and the Lemmon chuckle already on his lips.

But she didn't answer the door when he rang. To get in, he did what he had seen done a thousand times on the screen – broke down the door. Inside, he saw Millie lying across the bed. She was fully dressed in the outfit she had put on for her visit to her son's house. She had had a heart attack.

Memories come rushing back at moments like this, memories of one's own life and memories of what happened to other people when they were in similar situations. He remembered an actress with whom he once worked. She was supposed to play a woman who had just lost her mother. One night, just before the curtain went up, she was handed a telegram. It said that her own mother had just died. She went on stage in a stupor, living the very part she was being paid to play. When she came off, she was loudly chastised by the director – for playing the part too coolly, without any real conception of what the character would really be feeling.

As Jack contemplated his own bereavement, he thought of that evening. He decided Millie's death could not be allowed to have any effect on the way he did his work. 'I would never dream of using a personal tragedy to help my own performance,' he explained. 'I tend to shut out my own emotions. In fact, sometimes I have felt guilty at being able to do good work when I was emotionally troubled inside. I have wondered if I were callous.' That is a charge no one has yet levelled against him. If, however, he did not allow his emotions to show on screen, there were times when it was almost a miracle that they did not.

It wasn't the frequent tiffs with Felicia that bothered him. They *always* worked out all right, and if either of them did ever think of taking them seriously little Courtney was on hand for them to realize just how lucky they were. Jack's elder child, Chris, was another matter, however.

Jack didn't love him any the less, but there were clear signs of the generation gap at work as soon as Chris moved into his teens. Only a trained psychiatrist would be able to say what exactly went wrong. It could have been jealousy over Jack's new family; it could have been the break-up of Cynthia's second marriage. Both parents were finding the boy difficult to handle. When he was too old for the toys that had served as a bridge between them, Chris found it difficult to see anything in common between himself and his internationally famous father. It was a situation that caused Jack very great pain. There were problems with drugs. Between the time that Chris was fourteen and twenty, Jack didn't know how to relate to his son. It wasn't just a generation gap, more a generation chasm. 'I don't know where he went – to the moon, I think. He was on some other wavelength. That's all I know.' He would protest that it was never a serious rift, but the two had no idea how to communicate with each other, and as Lemmon himself said, without communication there could be no progress. 'All the attitudes are different . . . you try, all the love is there, and God knows, all the concern. But you just can't get on the same wavelength.'

But Jack tried. He took the boy on holiday with him. There was only one fast rule – no women present. They were going to live in the rough, and they didn't want any feminine influences protesting that they might get dirty or see some kind of unpleasant wild life. But these trips didn't help Jack to get to know his son or the son to understand his father. The gap just grew wider.

He had no doubt that his divorce from Cynthia had a great deal to do with it. He was trying too hard, hoping that he and Chris would become buddies, when both were wary of each other. Jack had had a remote relationship with his own father, and was going out of his way to make sure that it didn't happen in the new generation. When it did, he couldn't understand where he had gone wrong. Other parents have asked themselves the same questions and come up with no more obvious answers.

Meanwhile, he and Felicia were showing the world just how happy they really could be – once everyone else had accepted that they were living their own happy way. Certainly, he was doing well enough to keep her in the manner to which both of them felt they deserved to become accustomed. His own fees from *Cool Hand Luke* had been a million dollars plus ten per cent of the profits, which were now mounting up. He was persuaded to invest in oil wells. Five thousand of them, he claimed. The figure was not mentioned in a fit of bragging. On the contrary. 'Only one of 'em found a little poopin' gas or something,' he explained.

Everybody, it seemed, wanted to get in on the Jack Lemmon act. At the end of the 1960s Jack appeared in so many *Rowan and Martin Laugh-In* shows that it appeared that the programme was in danger of being called the *Jack Lemmon Laugh-In* – but the most significant development in his career was his decision to make another film with Walter Matthau.

The new Laurel and Hardy team cemented everything with *The Odd Couple*. They were like two lost friends who can't understand how they have got on without each other for so long. They may have begun to feel that way after *The Fortune Cookie*; after *The Odd Couple*, they were as sure of being blood brothers as if they had cut their thumbs and pressed them together.

All the chemistry that the two friends in Neil Simon's play of post-divorce mayhem did *not* have, Lemmon and Matthau developed for themselves by instinct. The fact that Matthau was almost as big a name as Lemmon made no difference to the concern and consideration that Jack showed him. There had, for instance, been talk of their swapping roles – Jack playing the untidy slob who acts as host to the neurotically neat writer whose wife has just left him bereft and lost in an outside world he barely knows exists. Walter had played the part of the slob on Broadway and done it phenomenally well. Jack wouldn't hear of their changing things.

Mike Nichols, the director, also wanted Matthau to keep to his old role. 'Walter,' he told him, 'you're born to this part.'

'And he was,' said Jack.

'Well,' Matthau told me, 'I had all the living I needed to do that role. It came very easily, very naturally. That is not to say I'm a naturally sloppy person. Nor am I a particularly neat person. I certainly know that kind of character. There's a kind of inner calm when you do something that works. You're kind of happy with it.'

Walder *did* look a slob. He couldn't be anything else, with a Christmas stocking still hanging on the hearth in midsummer and milk standing up on its own without a bottle in the refrigerator.

Jack played a pernickety man whose idea of hell was to see a piece of paper lying on the floor and not be able to do anything about it. In the film he was made to submit to all sorts of indignities – ranging from cigarette ash left on the floor by Matthau's card-playing buddies to tomato ketchup on the walls. He played the hypochondriac cold sufferer so well, you wanted to say 'bless you' every time he sneezed and to get up from your seat in the cinema to offer him a clean handkerchief. The relationship bears all the signs of a marriage gone wrong – but without the very slightest hint of homosexuality, latent or obvious, loving or hateful, which was an obvious risk.

The film succeeded because of the unusual way in which the two principals got on with each other. As Jack told me: 'Many, many actors – and ones that are good – don't work with you. They work *at* you. You can look them in the eye and yet they are not looking at you. When the other actor does look, that can be a magic moment.'

That was *The Odd Couple* – a film full of magic moments. *Time* magazine said it wasn't quite the perfect comedy film – because the camera tended to be too static. But, it said, *The Odd Couple* were 'real people, with enough substance to cast shadows alongside the jokes'. In other words, it worked, a fact that pleased Jack as much as almost anything else. He would say it was all because of his rapport with Walter. 'If in the middle of a scene someone gets an idea, there's no hesitation. We just do it.' He said it was a very lucky picture for him. It was indeed.

There were a lot of politicians who would have believed Jack Lemmon was a lucky person to have on their side. After all, it was a long-standing Hollywood tradition for the stars to rally around the big political figures of the age – and had been since President Franklin D. Roosevelt was greeted by a train-load of film people who came to Washington to speed along his campaign. Jack, however, remained aloof from most of that kind of thing. All his friends knew he was on the liberal wing of the Democratic party, but he wasn't one of those rushing around to be seen on platforms with the candidate, or to chair committees set up to plan inauguration balls.

In the late 1960s all eyes were on another former Hollywood actor, whose ambitions didn't seem to stretch much beyond the seemingly heady heights of the Governor's Mansion in Sacramento, California – Ronald Reagan. Even Jack, who never said a bad thing about anyone, found it difficult to be kind to his former colleague. 'There are three schools of thought about Reagan,' said Jack after he was elected. 'The first is that he is a man of great political acumen. The second that he has proved himself a better Governor than anyone thought he could be and third that he's just a great laugh. I'm somewhere between the second and third categories. I'll tell you how he got elected though. I was driving out to the studio on the day of the governorship primaries and it was about one o'clock and Reagan wasn't thought to be doing too well. And a news broadcast comes over the radio saying Reagan had publicly stated that if he did not win, he would definitely go back to his acting career. I laughed so much I almost had to stop the car. I could just imagine California, faced with that threat, rushing out immediately to vote for him.'

If anyone wanted to try to explain how Jack Lemmon became a superstar, the only explanation must be that he had the gift of surviving the disasters. It wasn't just that Jack himself treated failure with the kindness and consideration Billy Wilder mentions. He accepted it for himself with all the equanimity of a disappointed puppy who fails to get the bone. He just went on and sniffed for something new.

The April Fools was the bone he should have left behind. More cynical observers of the Hollywood scene could have concluded that the reason he didn't was that it would have meant giving up playing opposite one of the most beautiful women ever to have stood under the glare of a studio's lights, Catherine Deneuve, successor to Brigitte Bardot as both France's number-one sex-symbol and mistress of Roger Vadim. She played the girl with whom Jack eloped to Paris for the start of a distinctly unhappy marriage. No one could decide whether the film was meant to be funny or not, and it failed miserably to allay their doubts or make any money at the box office.

There were those who still hoped Jack would find a way back to television. In 1969 he did. But it was not in the kind of production he might have been expected to do. Instead he made a documentary, *The Slow Guillotine*, about the dangers of pollution to the environment. Jack narrated the piece and received the plaudits of the press for his contribution to society.

He wasn't the only one happy with his next role – live onstage for the first time since *Face of a Hero*. In a revival of the 1936 play *Idiot's Delight* at Los Angeles' Ahmanson Theatre, he himself was a delight. The play was by Robert E. Sherwood and directed by Garson Kanin, who promised Jack that he would make it seem as much like making a movie as possible – he would stand in the wings and yell 'Cut' whenever he thought it might be useful. As it turned out, he didn't need to use the word at all.

Jack was master of his new situation during the twelve-week run – a time when he could have commanded another full million dollars had he been using it for a film. He said he was frightened to ask his agent how much he would be getting for the role of Harry Van, an American song-and-dance man leading a troupe of girls, whose principal talent appeared to be located within the area encompassed by their bras, through Europe during the run-up to World War II. Jack was pleased to do the part because he saw this story of the gathering clouds of the late 1930s as being essentially an anti-war vehicle, and one that was much more effective than a more blatant contemporary piece. It was a part first portrayed on the stage by Alfred Lunt, and marked one of the less successful screen appearances of Clark Gable – who tried in vain to be convincing as a man who could tap his dancing shoes as effectively as he could thump women's hearts.

The play was made partly by the incidental characters, like the German scientist (brilliantly played by Sam Jaffe), the Italian army captain, the French Communist, and a couple of British honeymooners. Kanin was delighted to get Lemmon for the lead, as it virtually guaranteed a full-star supporting cast. 'I can ask anyone now,' said the director. He asked Rosemary Harris and she said yes.

There was one aspect of the play that Jack was keeping comparatively dark. He failed to reveal, until it was published in the programme, that he wrote all the music for the show himself. Audiences who didn't know about the other side to Jack's talents were somewhat surprised by the facility with which he played the piano on stage. The song and dance that he managed may not have put him in the Astaire class, but it certainly showed up the late Mr Gable's abilities for what they were – or rather what they were not.

The play was put on as part of the Center Theatre Group's third gala season. Before the first night, which was attended by such luminaries as Gregory Peck and Dyan Cannon, Jack received a telegram of good wishes from the first Van, Alfred Lunt, and his wife Lynn Fontanne, who told him they knew it would work well. They didn't say 'break a leg' – the most frequent showbiz greeting intended to provide exemption from all the other possible theatrical calamities – but the sentiment was there. There was one other greeting – from the same Ronald Reagan about whom Jack had had such profound doubts. The Governor was full of confidence for Jack's ability. He wrote: YOUR PARTICIPATION WILL I AM SURE ENCOURAGE OTHER STARS OF YOUR MAGNITUDE TO PARTICIPATE IN THIS FINE CIVIC ACTIVITY.

It was an important enough event for the play to be noticed throughout the United States. Mel Gussow wrote in the *New York Times* that Rosemary Harris played very well, but it wasn't really her play. 'It is left to Jack Lemmon to carry the play and he does. His performance alone is enough to make the revival worthwhile. Cocky but seedy in his checked suit and bow tie, he leads his six chorus girls through tired routines and leaves a trail of tired wisecracks all along the Balkan circuit. As he walks with a slight slouch, he is the perfect down-at-the-heels, up-to-the-mouth vaudevillian.' Mr Gussow was right in suggesting that the part of the good-humoured loser was not very different from the one he had played so many times since the days of *The Apartment*. 'It allows him to extract every ounce of humour, both light and biting, and the production is desperately in need of all the life that Lemmon can give it.' It was a back-handed compliment to the play, but to Jack they were the sweetest words he had heard about a stage performance of his own in years.

The next time audiences saw Jack he was in the more familiar surroundings of a cinema – in a film called *The Out-of-Towners*, about a married couple who come to the big city for a business interview, only to find that everything goes wrong. They can't get into an hotel, they are stranded in the rain . . . just the sort of thing that everyone knows happens to Jack Lemmon on the screen. In fact, it happened to Jack Lemmon off screen as well. He told me: 'When we went to Boston for part of the film, we got off the plane and found our luggage wasn't there. Now, we had gone there to do the film about getting off an aeroplane and no luggage. Sure enough, the luggage ended up in Kansas City. We were in Boston. We booked in at the Ritz Hotel and they said, "Who are you? We don't know you." It got to be midnight and we end up in three different hotels. No reservations. It was hysterical. I thought the producer had gone on ahead and that it was a put-on at first. He was jokey. I thought there would be cameras rolling, you know a kind of cinéma-vérité, but there weren't.'

Jack's wife in the film was played by Sandy Dennis, who was used to playing neurotic females in the midst of crises not of their own making. She had played with Jack once before – in *Face of a Hero*, which she has blotted from her memory bank even more successfully than has Jack. He may remember it as *Trace of a Zero* – she doesn't recall its title at all. Working with Jack in *The Out-of-Towners* represents a much happier memory entirely. 'I love him, if you can say that about someone you don't know well,' she told me. 'He is one of the most creative actors and pleasant people to be around I have ever met in my life.'

One of the problems of making the film was the weather in which the crew had to work. It was being filmed in March, with temperatures still sub-zero and snow all around. The script, however, said that it was autumn and that it was raining. 'We had, I remember, two enormous trucks full of water,' Sandy recalled. 'Jack decided that the best thing for him was to wear a wet suit under his clothes – I was much too vain to do that. I had my little skirt with my panty hose underneath. But when they poured the water over us, it froze. We had icicles on our hair. He caught the worst cold of all because he must have sweated inside. I didn't catch one at all.'

The film was another Neil Simon venture, as funny as one had by now come to expect any Simon vehicle would be. It was directed by Arthur Hiller. 'So many of the incidents had actually happened to people and Neil Simon had simply put them together,' Hiller told me. To him, Jack was sensational – both to work with and in the finished picture. 'When I say that, I'm talking in personal terms as well as acting terms. It's hard when people say such nice things about someone, but you can't say anything but nice things.' And he gave an example: 'There were crowds gathering around us. I've seen other actors in that position who quite rightly refuse to break up their work to give someone an autograph. Jack somehow managed to do it.'

Hiller told me, 'We were working at this stage in a busy street in Manhattan – so the police had to hold the traffic for about four blocks away for us. When you are doing that, you have to be able to say "Action" and the actors make their moves without any discussion. Jack was always ready to do it on time. I've often said that those two people, Jack and Sandy, could have taken three weeks longer to shoot that film without appearing to be destructive. But they worked it all out so that it wouldn't happen.'

The picture had a somewhat mixed reception, and what happened in England was fairly typical of the response it had everywhere. On the one hand, *The Times* reported: 'It is undoubtedly meant to be funny and at moments Neil Simon's script manages to extract some wry humour from the fearful trials his innocent visitors to New York encounter everywhere they go in the big city. But the sheer accumulation of misfortunes . . . soon becomes depressing.' The *Sunday Telegraph*, however, said just the opposite: 'It is a pity that the length of a review is invariably taken to be an indication of the quality of the product. Yet what more does one need to know about *The Out-of-Towners* than that it is a slight, gloriously funny-cruel Neil Simon comedy about a pair of innocents in a New York which is depicted as one huge booby-trap for the unwary. It is immaculately acted by Jack Lemmon and most surprisingly Sandy Dennis and is an object lesson for all the British comedies I have criticized lately which stuff themselves with box-office business to the exclusion of the bright idea that inspired them in the first place.'

If the film worked – and it is a jaundiced eye indeed that thinks it didn't – it worked because of Jack's total domination of the piece. Jack was everybody's idea of a fall guy. The amazing thing was that it never seemed like type-casting – even when the gap between his more serious ventures grew a little too long. In truth, most people preferred the man with the kind of problems everyone experiences but likes to keep quiet about. Things may happen to him as if by design, but you always want to find out what he is going to do next. Even when it seemed that a new role was just the old one rehashed, you sat back and waited for the surprise you knew was on the way.

In 1971, Jack surprised everyone by taking on a totally different role in a film with Walter Matthau. Once more, he let Walter have all the best scenes. It was obvious that he had to have them. In *Kotch*, Walter was the star. Jack was the director.

He had been hoping for an opportunity to direct for years. It was a need to express himself in a way that a thousand other actors who never get the chance would understand. Jack had the opportunity when his Jalem producer Richard Carter told him about a script he was trying to sell to a studio, about an old man who befriends an attractive young girl. Now that sounded like a very tired old idea indeed. Except that Mr Kotcher was like the girl's grandfather, who only wanted to get her to bed when she wasn't feeling well. And this girl wasn't feeling well at all. She was pregnant and had been thrown out of the same house as the old man. His own son and daughter-in-law, who employed the girl as a maid, wanted him out of the way. It tickled Jack's fancy. For a moment Carter was afraid he would want to play the lead himself, and turning Lemmon into a septuagenarian was even more difficult to imagine than having him dress up as a girl. No, Jack assured him, he wanted to be the director.

He even had a megaphone, complete with the initials J. L. in gold, on a shelf in his Jalem Productions office in Beverly Hills, just itching to be used. When the time came to start his first day's shooting, he admitted to quivering like a leaf. He was suffering, he revealed, from a distinct dose of 'unadulterated fear'. He just couldn't be sure how he would cope. For it was obvious, and he knew it, that an actor who *almost* lived every part he played in front of a camera wasn't going to be able to come home at the end of the day and forget what had happened in the previous ten hours or so. Felicia, who was to play the old man's uncaring daughter-in-law, knew it too.

What he was certain of was that Walter Matthau was the man to play Mr Kotcher. The star, who in *Plaza Suite* – yet another Neil Simon product – had already played a film producer, a hassled businessman and a father who splits his tailcoat trying to persuade his daughter to come out of the bathroom for her wedding, couldn't have much trouble with a tall old man with steel-rimmed spectacles and a panama hat.

The story had been peddled around for years. Carter had at one time hoped that Spencer Tracy might do the part, but he died before anything could be settled. He then tried Fredric March, who wanted to do it very much indeed. But March, after a lifetime as a top star, was no longer considered bankable. So Walter was produced and the *Seven Year Itch* problem was reversed. He wanted the part – and wanted Jack to direct.

'Well,' Jack told me when I met him as he planned this new operation from the offices of what had become his subsidiary company (called, inevitably, Kotch Productions), 'if it works, it is because Walter and I respect each other and can anticipate how the other is going to react.' It was a fact yet to be proved – but the proof came. Jack had only to suggest an idea and Walter responded. 'Gotcha,' said Walter.

Directing, Jack told me, was something he had to get out of his system. But *Kotch* came first; if he hadn't been offered that particular film, he would have waited till one that matched his directing potential came along. 'In reading the script, I found myself reading it not as an actor, but as a director. I saw it before me and thought this was something I could do as a director, which good, bad or indifferent would be *my* film. At least, I saw a way to do it that was unique – my point of view.' But there were problems. 'You have to be careful. I think one of the traps that directors fall into is directing everybody in the same manner. If you're smart, you take your time and figure what's the best way you can reach so-and-so as opposed to reaching Lemmon or Matthau or whomever. I've seen it happen over and over again; a marvellous director speaking to an intelligent actor, and nobody's home. The guy is listening, but he doesn't know what the hell the director is talking about, because the director hasn't realized that's not how you're going to get to this guy.'

But even though it took a year out of his life, it was an ambition fulfilled – and just fired his desire to do it some time again. 'I think the desire to direct is at the back of every actor's mind. That is probably because – in my case it turned out to be true – it is more creative and less interpretative, and especially in this medium. On the stage, there is nothing you can do about a play once the curtain has gone up. It's in the hands of the actors and the gods. In film that is not so. You can retake, redo. And then you have the editing, the dubbing, and where you are putting your camera. Everything is really one man's point of view – and it is the director's view. You have to have the bricks and the mortar through talks with the writers and the cameramen, but it is the director's house you are building. I guess for one's own ego, there is that itch.' Now he was seeing things from the director's point of view he could also unload the frustrations he had himself experienced when directors didn't see things his own way. Lemmon, of course, had been lucky with many of his directors – Wilder and Quine, for instance, who would no more have upset Jack than they would have forgotten to put film in their cameras.

But even he confessed to me that this did enter into it. 'Any actor will tell you that along with the good times there have been those when he has worked with a very restrictive director, or at least one who won't allow the actor to at least try what he sees, the ideas that he gets, the inspiration that he has.'

That wasn't the kind of director he intended to become. 'Those are the most insecure directors. The most secure directors are the kind who don't give the ultimate direction of what to do at all times.' Although he thought he would be frustrated at not doing the acting, that wasn't what happened. 'There is immense satisfaction in having your own ideas, giving them to another actor and seeing his eyes light up when it works.' What was difficult was the exhaustion that he felt. At three o'clock in the afternoon he was finished, because at no time had he been off his feet. As an actor in a picture, he only had to think of his own part. Now he had to think of the whole – and when everyone else was relaxing, he had to bother with camera angles and cutting points.

Filming began in Palm Springs on a tramway. It wasn't as simple as he had been led to believe. 'It was madness,' he said at the time. 'We had been assured complete freedom to use the tram, which wasn't true. We had been misinformed about the sun. It disappeared behind peaks from time to time during the morning. And people on the tram were starting to get seasick.'

He had the advantage of his experience as an actor. He understood that there were also actors' problems and knew how to approach an actor. The trap was expecting another actor to play it the way Jack would play it. 'I had seen other actors who became directors do that, and I tried to avoid it for myself. Not because a performance might be bad, but because he should create an atmosphere in which actors feel very free to bring all that they can.'

But more than anything else he enjoyed what he did. As he told me: 'I've had the biggest boot in my entire career making this film. If the film is a failure I'll still feel that way.'

He cut very little, by most directors' standards. First he took out thirty minutes, then he put five minutes back. After the film's preview in San Diego, another twenty-two seconds were excised. The film went down so well that the theatre reported virtually no sales of popcorn during the showing and no one left to go to the lavatories – which Jack L. Warner had always decided was the best guide to a movie's success. (The lavatory yardstick never let him down. 'It's no good,' he said on one occasion as he gave the thumbs down to a preview. 'It was a two-piss picture.') Later, it did good business at New York's Radio City Music Hall, but it wasn't acclaimed by every critic who saw it.

The *New York Times* led its film review page with Vincent Canby's assessment of the picture – a fact usually heralding a paean if not of praise then certainly of appreciation. Mr Canby, however, didn't like *Kotch* at all: 'Lemmon's ability as a director must be judged, I think, as much by the material with which he chose to make his début, as by the end product. Both are so unadventurous as to be downright depressing.'

But it *was* a picture with a bittersweet taste that benefited by the touch of Lemmon. The pity was that it wasn't a big enough hit to make him rush back to the director's chair and pick up that megaphone again. He hasn't directed another movie since. As far as audiences were concerned, Jack Lemmon was an actor – and they felt cheated not to *see* him in any film with which his name was associated.

The early 1970s weren't a fertile time. In fact, Hollywood had rarely been in worse shape. As a producer he decided to 'hold out' until something really suitable came along, suitable enough for a time when, as he put it, 'business was very tight'.

The answer, he decided, was *The War Between Men and Women*, in which Jack peered through pebble-thick spectacles in a role based firmly on the latter years of humorist James Thurber's life. The story was of a writer who – like Thurber himself – was going blind. In the outer office of his eye specialist he trips over the shapely legs of another patient (played by Barbara Harris) who, like him, is wearing thick black glasses. Her eye trouble is minimal – although she can't be sure that the same can be said for this man who has so suddenly entered her life. For one thing, it wasn't usual for a total stranger to grab her left breast as this man was doing while trying to support himself against one of her thighs. A little while later she meets him again, and before long finds herself matching his fantasies of getting her into bed.

Eventually – after competing for attention with her children, her pregnant dog (which gives birth in the middle of a busy Manhattan roadway) and her first husband – he marries her.

Not everyone shares my own view that in this picture the true genius of Jack Lemmon came to the fore, but it was certainly one of his best. The animation in the midst of the 'battle' scene when Jack and Jason Robards (as the first husband) let loose their anti-feminist frustrations, and then when the Thurberesque character tells the story of the 'Little Flower', were the best of their kind since Jerry the mouse danced with Gene Kelly in *Anchors Aweigh*.

Jack said that it was due in no small part to the director, Melville Shavelson, who also co-wrote it with the producer, Danny Arnold. Shavelson is the first to say that he didn't come up with *The War Between Men and Women* simply as a Jack Lemmon vehicle. They had first met soon after Max Arnow brought Jack to Hollywood and stayed friends the way Hollywood people did – meeting at the same parties, acknowledging each other at the times that Hollywood people get together. They also had the same agent, who gave Jack the script to read. Shavelson told me that Jack had read the script all night and then asked, 'Do you think they will let me do it?' He was very excited about the script, particularly when he found out that it had been gathering dust at Warner Brothers, where Shavelson had once worked, and which had now rejected it.

It was in many ways the fulfilment of a pipe-dream for Shavelson. He had previously created a television series based on Thurber's stories called *My World and Welcome to It*, which won an Emmy award and then was cancelled by networks who are kept alive by money from advertisers, not by praise from art-loving critics. *The War Between Men and Women* was another crack at Thurber's world, but Shavelson had not envisaged Jack Lemmon as the star, nor had he seen it as a feature-length picture. Shavelson had originally planned to turn the story into a stage musical, but when Jack came along and showed an almost passionate interest in the project, there were no doubts that this was the way it had to go.

'Jack worked amazingly hard,' said Shavelson. 'But he also relaxed – by taking a few too many drinks, although never too many that he lost control.' A lot of the filming took place on California's Catalina Island, which was meant to double for Long

Island, New York. 'Jack and Jason Robards would drink martinis incessantly,' he recalled. 'One night they walked home with each other after having a few too many. One of them fell into a garbage can. The other tried very hard – and not very satisfactorily – to lift him out of it.' He either couldn't remember or didn't want to say which function was reserved for which actor. It was a difficult time for both men. Jack was in the midst of his crisis with Chris, and Jason Robards 'had problems I didn't know about,' said Shavelson. A very short time afterwards, Jason's car collided with a telegraph pole and he was almost killed.

Jack was at an age when he had to decide to change from the kind of comedy role in which he had luxuriated since *Some Like It Hot* and before. *The War Between Men and Women* was a comedy of bad manners, a muse that had its sad moments but the only time you wanted to cry was when the laughs, usually so subtle, made you need to laugh even more.

The scenes involving animation required a greater discipline than even an actor of Jack Lemmon's standing was used to. He had to do everything in front of a screen while the images of the animated characters were being projected around him. Because it was front projection, the kind every cinema or home movie addict uses, he couldn't move too much, or the images would be projected on to the back of his shirt. But he managed it. Every movement that Jack made in the film – from the initial fall and grab at the more intimate parts of Barbara Harris's anatomy – was rehearsed again and again to get just the right, shall we say, feel. Jack is not on record as protesting, nor is Barbara Harris. Before the lighting of the cigarette, over which they have to fumble in their world of darkness, was achieved, they had to repeat the action again and again.

Shavelson discovered what Billy Wilder and all the other directors had known all along. It was easy to direct Jack because when he made suggestions they were useful ones. If the director wanted him to do something, he didn't object. As he told me: 'Jack's one of *the* most professional actors, who takes his comedy very seriously. So certain is he of his talent, that he doesn't have to impress you by demanding changes.'

As with most of his other pictures, the name Jack Lemmon was more than just an insurance policy for National General, who went into partnership with Jalem to make the movie. It was more like a cast-iron endowment. The man who didn't like to consider himself a businessman had already sold television rights – so that the money he got from the television networks covered the immediate costs of the negative and the movie was in profit the moment it first threaded its way through cinema projectors. 'We all benefited from that,' said Shavelson. 'He insisted that we should all get the same deal that he got.' In the light of some of the slating that the film received, that was fortunate.

Jack's policy was to try to forget what the critics had said and get on with his next project – although he had by now discovered a new diversion that was beginning to rival not just his pool-playing, but even his addiction to the piano. Jack became a golfer – although he wasn't as good on the links as he would like to think he was. As the years progressed, so would his golf – not in performance but in his determination to master the game the way other stars did.

The piano *was*, however, still there, and in May 1972 he won an Emmy himself for a television show in which he wasn't required to do more than play his favourite keyboard. The show was *S'wonderful, S'marvellous, S'Gershwin* – and with Jack at the piano it was all these things. It delighted practically everyone who saw it, but succeeded in mystifying all those people who believed that Jack Lemmon was an actor. So he had to regain his principal constituency, especially now that he was being regarded as something of a fixture in Hollywood life. As the magazine *Films in Review* reported: 'Not a few knowledgeable people think the one successor to Bob Hope the American people will wholeheartedly accept is Jack Lemmon.'

Now there was a new film to work on which would reveal yet another facet of the Jack Lemmon career – his first nude scene. Jack in the buff was not a pretty sight. Juliet Mills, his co-star, was no Raquel Welch either, but both stripped off for the cameras because, as people in the industry used to say in the mid-1970s, the story demanded it. In this case, Billy Wilder demanded it and Jack didn't argue with Billy now any more than he had in their previous pictures.

Actually, Jack doesn't want the significance of this event to be over-emphasized, although in a way he argues against that philosophy. 'There wasn't really a nude scene,' he insisted a little while later. And that, he added with his characteristic insouciance, was almost a pity: 'I have, in my opinion, the cutest tushy in show business.'

The film was *Avanti*, and this time it was set in Italy. Jack played an incredibly rich American, desperately awaiting the death of his industrialist father so that he can take over the family concern. The girl was the daughter of an English manicurist. They came together when both arrived at the Italian seaside resort frequented by their parents, who – surprise, surprise – they discover have been carrying on an illicit romance for years. Before long, as one might expect in such a film, that was precisely what would happen to Jack and Juliet, which sounded more like a nursery rhyme than the rest of the story.

Jack was the first to admit that he was disappointed in *Avanti*. As he later explained to the *Chicago Tribune*: 'In the old days, my generation thought of movies as escapist entertainment where stars would sell tickets even if the films were lousy. That's no longer true. I can't make *Avanti* a success if it's no good. This is healthy.'

That, of course, was usually Jack's story, too. You believed in the people he played because he *was* lifelike. Suddenly in 1973, it was all getting *too* lifelike. In his next film he was expected to save a tiger. It seemed, however, that what really needed saving was Jack Lemmon.

8

Save the Tiger

What Jack didn't know when he signed to make a film called *Save the Tiger* was that it would be so important in his life. Not just in his career, although it would be a milestone, but in his life. Afterwards, he recognized he had been fairly close to a breakdown without realizing it.

What saved him, he said, was Felicia and the rest of his family. There were still problems with Chris, and still fights at home, but Jack could take them. They still made each other laugh, which counted for a great deal. She was, meanwhile, debating whether or not she could bear to give up her career if it ever crossed with that of her husband. So far it hadn't. While Jack was working out details for *Save the Tiger* she was planning her next movie with her rival for Jack's affections, Walter Matthau, in *Charley Varrick*.

Felicia had decided that if it came to the crunch, she would have to be the one to give way. That was partly because Jack was the bigger star, but also, because she was, she said, 'part of the old mould of women who believe that marriage, after all, comes first. And I wouldn't want to leave Jack or the children for any length of time.'

Jack had reason enough to need her when he played the part of Harry Stoner in *Save the Tiger*, a performance almost completely bereft of laughs, but one for which it now looked as though *Days of Wine and Roses* had served as an extremely useful apprenticeship. It had been a part that had preyed on his imagination for three years in a way he could never have imagined. Certainly not when the idea was first offered to him by the writer, Steve Shagan.

At the time he said, 'I was making *April Fools*, when this guy comes up to me and says would I like to read this script and how he's going to haunt me till I do. So I ask him what he's done before and he says he was associate producer on the Tarzan series which, I have to confess, does not make me feel like saying. "Oh boy, I can't wait to read this." However, I did read it. And after the first scene, I'm hooked. It's so realistic, so honest. It didn't have the smell of cold Hollywood.'

It wasn't the Jack Lemmon anyone expected to see, although in this film, which dwelt on a mere twenty-four hours in the life of a Los Angeles dress manufacturer, he had never looked better. He wore a smart silk suit – so smart and so silky that three characters in the film refer to it – and his silvering hair gave him an air of authority that would have convinced anyone to buy his dresses, if he wasn't a man of such loose integrity. His products are undoubtedly great. He and his partner, a beautiful character study by Jack Gilford of an older man for whom success and riches have not let him forget the New York East Side, have never had a more commercial line. But they are up to their coat-hangers in debt and Stoner decides that the only way he can escape from his problems is to arrange to have one of his factories burnt down so that they can collect the insurance money.

In the street, outside the cinema where the arson deal is confirmed with a specialist in such things, he is importuned to 'save the tiger'. He knows that he himself is an equally endangered species if he goes ahead with his plans but can't see any other alternative. The only thing that this character and Jack himself had in common was the concentration they awarded to their work – and their mutual love of music. Stoner begins his day playing tapes of swing music. He continues the recitals in his car – and he is too concerned with the problems of the coming day to be attracted by a girl who invites him 'to ball' although he does meet the girl again quite casually at the end of the day. Once more, it was a case of Jack stepping into his character's handmade shoes. Only this time it took on a seriousness that had never occurred before. He needed empathy with every character he played.

Jack and I discussed that just a few months after *Save the Tiger* was released. People had asked him, he said, how he could like a character who was so totally devoid of ethics. 'I told them that it was not important that I *liked* the character I played. What was very important was that I cared about him and understood him. I didn't agree with anything that the character believed in or one word that he said, but I never cared about a character more. That's the difference, I think.'

He took the dress manufacturer home with him in the evenings in a way even the alcoholic or the unwilling transvestite had never gone home. Worse, he travelled with him to and from the studio. He would be driving down Sunset Boulevard when, for no apparent reason, tears would cascade down his cheeks. He didn't know why – he would just suddenly weep and there was nothing he could do to control it.

'Then I realized it was the nutty guy I was playing,' he said. He returned to the house at night to be greeted by Felicia with the announcement: 'The loony's home!' Well, after that, even a man close to a nervous breakdown had to laugh. But much of the rest of the time he was worried, if not about Chris, who no longer felt he had to prove anything to his father, then about the guy he so readily understood was having all those difficulties amid the sewing and cutting machines of his factory. That was once the film was actually being made. Before then, there had been problems of a totally different kind.

Practically every studio in Hollywood had been asked to put up the money for the picture and turned it down. Eventually Paramount came in with Jalem, Filmways and Cirandinha. Steve Shagan, the young man who had had the original idea, and who wrote the screenplay, was the producer. This was his big chance both to say something and to have an international star fronting his product. The biggest obstacle was simply that the business brains of Hollywood did not believe the public would want to go to theatres showing a film about the problems of a middle-aged businessman. As Jack has said since then: 'At that time, they still felt that three-quarters of the movie-going audience was thirty or under. Rightly or wrongly, they felt that younger people wouldn't care. They all respected the script, but they just didn't feel there

was an audience.' Hence Jack's decision to work for a 'scale' fee
– the Equity minimum, which at the time was about $165 a
week.

Actually, there were other reasons why studios were showing
all the enthusiasm of a polar bear lost in the Sahara. Hollywood
had always been a centre for American flag-waving – the
immigrant moguls had decided that films were the ideal means
of demonstrating affection for their new country as well as of
unloading their inferiority complexes in a massive display of
assimilation – and that patriotism still lingered. The men sitting
behind the big studio desks were worried that the critique of
American morals which *Save the Tiger* represented was nothing
less than an attack on their beloved nation.

Just as many thought the film was anti-Semitic. The extraordinarily sympathetic roles of Jack's partner and of the holocaust survivor, who divided his time between chain-smoking
and being the most outstanding pattern-cutter in the American
garment industry, were undeniably Jewish. No one said that the
amoral Harry Stoner was, too, but it was a reasonable assump-
tion. Others said the film was Communist propaganda.

Before all this, there had been some interest abroad. A Paris
studio wanted François Truffaut to direct it with Yves Montand
in the Stoner role. Jack's conviction that it would be a brilliant
movie made in Hollywood was what finally sold the deal.

Shagan had written the story out of hot-blooded anger, but it
took him more than two years to complete the script. When it
was finally ready to go before the cameras, the director John
Avildsen insisted on filming it both on location in the less
salubrious areas of Los Angeles and in sequence. Normally that
is a recipe for economic disaster, but he was certain that this
particular film needed the extra flow of adrenalin that Harry
Stoner's problems *in situ* provided.

The search for reality went too far for even Jack. Because the
deal for the arson attempt is struck in a cinema, the director
insisted on using a real picture theatre – one of the pseudo
classical palaces built in the 1930s and now eking out a seedy
existence showing blue movies. And because he wanted the
degradation being suffered by the men from the garment factory

to be emphasized, Avildsen wanted a real film to be shown on the screen as the men talk to their arsonist.

That was too much. Jack asked him to stop the film and dub the soundtrack later – audiences could hear the dialogue, mostly a holier-than-thou commentary on the need for sexual freedom, while the conspirators talked. With a real film being shown, Jack found himself constantly looking at the screen – he had never seen a blue movie before. 'Here I was, trying to be disturbed, secretive and frightened while watching one girl making love to another girl with a peach, and then this guy walks in . . . '

Jack saw Harry Stoner as more than just a 'good character' who was worth acting. It was almost as though he were playing him on behalf of all his countrymen. 'Harry Stoner is the whole, middle-stream American prototype. He fought in World War II and nobody even remembers it. If we look at our society, there is nothing left a young man coming out of that war can still believe in. We accept Watergate. We accept Vietnam. We accept cheating on our income tax and dancing around the law. We accept junkies knifing us in the streets. We accept the injustices in our courts. There are no rules, just referees. We used to salute the flag. Now they're making jockstraps out of it.'

Early on, it looked certain to be a different sort of film. If he hadn't won an Oscar for years, it was more that his pictures weren't the type that usually attracted Academy awards than a refusal to recognize his talent. Now a film of Oscar quality was matching his usual Oscar performance. Unfortunately, he was taking it all too seriously – off screen as well as on.

Felicia has described him as almost a man of dual personality. The loving father and husband was not Harry Stoner at home, but he was a total neurotic. He snapped at everyone around him. Some nights he found it easier not to talk at all. 'I was so distraught,' he said, 'I couldn't shake it. I couldn't relate to anything else. I couldn't give a damn about anything else. I was too far into this role and I was afraid of losing Harry Stoner.'

What Felicia was afraid of losing was Jack Lemmon. His tears while driving became such a problem that she now drove him to work in the morning. He was talking to himself, which could have been a further attempt at understanding Stoner, but no one could be sure. 'If Felicia had not been an actress and understood what I was going through,' Jack told me, 'I really think she might well have packed up and left.' The entire household suffered. Courtney, who adored her father, was totally mystified as to why he now found it virtually impossible to play their favourite games together at the end of the day.

I told Jack that I was always struck by the similarity that undoubtedly existed between the man on screen and the one I had interviewed. 'I'm delighted to hear that,' he said. 'I can't close the door of the shop at six and go home and forget it – especially certain parts that are more demanding.'

When *Save the Tiger* was completed and both Jack and the director John Avildsen were satisfied, the pressures eased – although they stayed until the reviews started appearing. Only then could Jack afford to relax. He was in New York when the film opened on the West Coast. Felicia read him the reviews.

Rex Reed in the *Los Angeles Times* said: 'It is one of the best films ever to come out of the Hollywood studios and it's unquestionably the summit of Jack Lemmon's acting career.' In the same paper Charles Champlin wrote: 'It is much the best thing Lemmon has ever done, which is saying a great deal if you remember only *The Apartment* and *Days of Wine and Roses*.' In the *Herald Examiner*, it was a similar story. Richard Cuskelly said : 'Lemmon's Harry is one of those hair-raising gut performances that have a life far outside the time and span of the film.'

It was the same all over the United States and abroad. In London, the *Sunday Express*'s Clive Hirschhorn wrote: '*Tiger* shows how American values have changed in the last twenty-five years. . . . There's no denying Jack Lemmon's stunning performance or the skill with which the film had been made.'

'Aren't they great?' Felicia asked after she had finished reading the papers over the phone.

'Just wonderful!' he replied.

'You're right,' she said. 'But I'm not sure that it was worth it.'

The only sour note was struck by *Time* magazine, whose sole comment about Jack was that he was 'less febrile here than usual'. As for the film, the magazine's critic Jay Cocks said: 'Director John Avildsen, who made *Joe*, continues to prove himself a master of the visual cliché, the low-slung symbol and the stereophonic anti-climax. He is abetted by scenarist Steve Shagan, a sort of drip-dry Clifford Odets, who puts klieg lights around every metaphor.' Mr Cocks was to be proved gloriously wrong.

This demanding part celebrated a milestone in the story of Jack Lemmon. He had finally come to terms with himself – or, as he put it, 'in my mid-forties, I had finally got out of puberty. I stopped chastising myself for my faults and said, "Screw it – that's me". I have faults and I can live with them. I finally began to like myself. Ultimately, I found that I was adorable!'

Sometimes his extra-studio work looked demanding, too. I met Jack at his office in El Camino Drive the day before he was due to go into hospital for a hernia operation. He was charming and tried to joke, but he was anxious about the next day – as perhaps only someone who had been in hospital so many times in his childhood could be. He talked about it a number of times. That night we met again. It was the evening of the American Film Institute's presentation of its Life Achievement award to James Cagney. Jack was to speak, to pay tribute to the actor and dancer who had taught him so much, and whom he admired greatly.

When Jack's turn was called, he mounted the rostrum and looked around him, all the usual confidence on his countenance. He began to tell the story about Cagney spotting his use of his left hand – and got lost. He talked and he talked. But practically nothing made sense. His sentences were long and rambling and didn't appear to get anywhere. As he admitted afterwards: 'When I heard my voice coming out of me, my mind was working, but I couldn't speak straight. It was a nightmare.'

Towards the end, film-maker Sam Peckinpah shouted words of abuse at Jack and was escorted from the banqueting suite at the Century Plaza Hotel where the ceremony was taking place. Jack continued to ramble till he was persuaded to leave. There was consternation in the hall. Outside, a few minutes later, I heard Shirley MacLaine say to friends: 'Whatever happened to Jack tonight? Have you ever heard him like that before?'

Nobody had. Lemmon had returned to his table to face a glaring Felicia. He was bewildered, too. He didn't know what had happened to him. She told him he was terrible. When he got angry, Felicia poured a glass of water on her husband's head. Most of the other guests had by that time left.

Later, both Felicia and Jack realized what had happened. He had been taking pills all day in readiness for his visit to hospital – and, at the same time, had been drinking. At the Cagney dinner he was drinking white wine. The booze and the pills didn't mix at all well. But, like the occasional disappointments in his career, no one held it against him. The operation was performed and he quickly recovered from that, too. The mixture of Jack Lemmon and Harry Stoner was, however, a lot more potent. And he was aware of it. 'A part does take over a little and you take over a little. There is a union wherein the part would not exist and you wouldn't exist were it not for that union. I find the acting process very difficult. My great problem is to make it seem easy.'

In *Save the Tiger* it didn't seem easy. It looked hard only because Harry Stoner was suffering so much. You suffered as you watched him. The Academy of Motion Picture Arts and Sciences obviously thought so too. For *Save the Tiger*, Jack Lemmon was awarded his second Oscar, his first as Best Actor.

It hadn't been a foregone conclusion, although earlier in the day he had begun to worry about the possibility. A clairvoyant on a television show had predicted that Jack would win by a landslide – and then added for good measure that one of the reasons for his assured success was that he had been the King of Thailand in a previous life. So many people rang him with their virtual guarantee that he was home and dry that he started thinking of it as the kiss of death. Being such a popular Hollywood figure, and having failed to get the award before, the talk was that Jack would win it for sentimental reasons. He didn't want those reasons to be the deciding factor. In the end, the probability was that they were not. There were too many other good actors hoping to walk off with the 1974 statuette to make that at all likely.

His competitors were Marlon Brando for *Last Tango in Paris*, Al Pacino for *Serpico*, Jack Nicholson for *The Last Detail* and the heir to all the Hollywood male glamour figures of the past, Robert

Redford for his part in *The Sting*. All but Brando were not just younger than Lemmon but were part of the new Hollywood wave that made him look an old-timer – after all, he had been making films now for twenty years. Las Vegas was making him a 3–1 favourite.

He had been nervous all day. When he greeted reporters at his door with a mug of coffee in one hand and an obvious shake in the other, only the fact that he was too busy taking calls could explain why he wasn't reacting even more excitedly. 'Hell,' he told them, 'I haven't even thrown up yet.'

The only time he hadn't had a severe attack of nerves on Oscar day was the one year when he was nominated and was out of the country. The atmosphere didn't get to him then. The only distraction was the fact that he had a speech to make, when he presented a special Oscar to Groucho Marx. As for a message of thanks for an award of his own, he kept going back to the time of the Cagney presentation – and, he said, he had even dreamed the night before of being interrupted by Sam Peckinpah.

This time, he was lucky. It *was* the name of Jack Lemmon that was called and it was his turn to look into the eyes of his wife and give her a big kiss (and another one for his co-star Jack Gilford). Later, when reporters asked him why he thought he had won, Walter Matthau called out, 'because he's the best.' Felicia said the Oscar was like having a baby. 'No,' she corrected herself, 'like having twins.'

Columnist Joyce Haber rejoiced in the win. She saw Jack as the direct descendant of Chaplin and Keaton and said it was the first time a 'true comedian' had won a top Oscar. Jack wouldn't have thanked her for the title but was doubtless grateful for the compliment – even though he had never played less of a comedy role in his life.

When the statuette was firmly in his hands, Jack reflected on what it all meant to him. 'There has been a great deal of criticism about this award,' he said after collecting the bronze Oscar from Liza Minnelli, 'but justified or not, I think it's one hell of an honour and I'm thrilled.' The Oscar proved that there were other things in life than money, although *Save the Tiger*, with the award behind it, did well enough at the box office and there were profits for Jack to scoop up – sufficient reward for his faith and persistence.

There were also other prizes. The Academy elected him a governor and even *Avanti* produced recognition. The Hollywood Foreign Press Association awarded him a Golden Globe for Best Supporting Actor. His old college, too, showed its appreciation of the glory in which it could reflect after his triumph. The Hasty Pudding Club gave him their Man of the Year award 'for his outstanding achievement in film acting and directing'. It was not a view universally held at that educational establishment. The Harvard *Lampoon* was less than kind to its old boy. It said it was giving Jack the 'Kirk Douglas Award for Worst Actor of the Year'. The 'Natalie Wood Worst Actress Award' went to Barbra Streisand for *The Way We Were*, which didn't do badly in terms of critical or box office acclaim either.

Save the Tiger had to be seen as a modern morality play – or immorality, for the distinct impression is given that Stoner is going to get away with his arson. But certainly there were messages there, and he took them round the country with him. He even discussed the film well into the night with students at Yale – which fellow Harvard men might consider close to high treason – giving his 'lectures' much of the intensity he had given to Harry Stoner, and appearing for breakfast later that morning with a look on his face as heavy as the subject for discussion. It took three Bloody Marys and a dish of eggs to bring him back to some semblance of life. He repeated the experience at college campuses all over the country.

He took the film to London, too, showing Courtney round Hyde Park, and going to the theatre every evening with Felicia – and usually offering his congratulations to the star. (It was an oft-repeated gesture. In New York, he was so impressed by Alan Bates' performance in *Butley* that he gave a party for him with a guest list including the Gregory Pecks, Jean Simmons, Richard Brooks and Lee Marvin.) In the day he was mostly marooned in his penthouse suite – 'the advantage with penthouses is that you get the breeze' – talking to British reporters about *Save the Tiger*, which, he was now saying, was relevant to all that he believed about ecology! Anyway, London was the most civilized city in the world and if he couldn't get his message across there, he never would. When people said that what they really wanted to hear was how he made his films, he obliged with a lecture at the National Film Theatre. Jack had never worked so hard on promoting a film before, but he felt it was worth it because he had never loved a picture as much.

The awards tumbled in like leaves marking the passage of time in an old black-and-white Hollywood montage. With Faye Dunaway he was nominated by the National Association of Theatre Owners as one of the Stars of the Year – for 'professional excellence and box-office popularity'. It was both a tribute to Jack's talent and a word of thanks to a couple of players who had helped to keep them in business. But that had been Jack's last motive in *Save the Tiger*; he had seen it as the fulfilment of his dream to enlighten as well as to entertain. He had done it brilliantly, and it rescued the reputation of a film industry that some thought inextricably bogged down in the mire of mediocrity.

Lemmon is transparently among the restless souls of Hollywood. Whereas Walter Matthau told me one of the great delights of being a successful film star was that he only had to work for twenty weeks of the year, Jack could never be content without work, or at least plans of work to come.

Every now and again those plans would turn to playing – a better word than 'working' to describe what they did together – with Walter. In 1973 they had two such ideas to go on. One was a new film with Billy Wilder, a remake of the Charles MacArthur–Ben Hecht newspaper story *The Front Page*. The other was a stage play, the Sean O'Casey canvas of the Irish troubles, *Juno and the Paycock*.

It wasn't just that Jack and Walter got on so well and enjoyed so much the thrust and parry of working with each other, but Jack liked being with people whose acting he admired, and Walter, with his hangdog expression and diction that seemed to have been polished on the way back from a union meeting, fitted snugly into that category. When we met on the eve of starting work on *The Front Page* – the third version to date (the second had been *His Girl Friday*) – Jack was saying that Walter was a man to be envied. 'I've always been jealous of Walter because he finds the whole process of acting much easier than I do, which would be fine if he wasn't all that good. But he happens to be sensational.'

Neither the critics nor Billy Wilder thought that *The Front Page* was sensational, which is a pity because Jack gave a beautiful portrayal of the reporter torn between the joint pressures of passion in his heart and ink in his veins. As in both previous versions, the story was hilariously funny, with Walter as the city editor milking every possible opportunity to get the reporter back to work and away from the girl planning to drag him off on honeymoon.

If success in a film is believing that nobody else could possibly have played those parts, then this *Front Page* triumphed. The trouble appears to have been that too many people still believed that the reporter looked like Pat O'Brien and the editor was Adolphe Menjou – the men who played the roles in the 1931 version, a film which had persuaded a whole generation of youngsters to become newspapermen. There were not just marvellous verbal duels between Hildy Johnson and Mr Burns, his city editor, but there was the atmosphere of the filthy press-room at the court building, the bottles of whisky, the phones, the messages on the wall, the pictures. There was the cameo from David Wayne of the arty-effeminate reporter worried about others using his toilet roll, and Carol Burnett as the prostitute who exposed her heart every time she went down on her back.

Billy Wilder told me that he was convinced it was a mistake to remake the picture and would never take that risk again. '*The Front Page* was a poor picture,' he said with assurance – only a man who had achieved so much else could afford to be so scathing about his own achievements. 'Only a fool would involve himself in remaking something that has gone down in history as an "immortal masterpiece". It was a fairly good play at the time, but they remember it being much better than it actually was when it was a smash on Broadway and as a movie. I will not do those things again. I will not remake anything – it is like trying to repaint the ceiling of the Sistine Chapel.'

I wondered whether Wilder and Lemmon had come to a joint decision on that when they held their post mortem on the film. The answer was that they didn't hold any post mortem. 'When we make a picture that doesn't work, we never talk about it – in fact, we rarely talk about films we have done at all. We talk about films we may make, about what is in our future. We don't retrace our glories or our flops. But we talk about other things – about golf, about how sad it is to get older with all those pretty girls coming up, we talk about music, we talk about the theatre. But most of all, we talk about sports. We watch football together, tennis.'

They have homes near each other and when both are in residence they often find the opportunity to meet. 'It's no fun watching a football game with a small bet on it and screaming with no one to hear you,' said Wilder. 'If we root for the same teams, we scream together. If we support opposing teams, we scream at each other.' Frequently they are on the same side – supporting local teams like the Rams in American football or the Dodgers in baseball. 'When there's an American playing at Wimbledon, we support him – unless it's John McEnroe and then we are both against him.'

Together they went to the Los Angeles surgery of Dr Chen, a Chinese specialist in acupuncture. Jack was suffering from an intensely painful tennis elbow, Wilder had problems with his back. Both were delighted with the results. 'It really is the funniest thing,' Jack said. 'The two of us lying side by side on slabs and this little Chinese doctor, quite brilliant he is, sticking pins into us and talking in an accent we can hardly understand.'

Wilder thought he had the answer. '*Sprechen Sie Deutsch*?' he asked. As Jack said: 'I'd have doubled up laughing if I didn't have the pins in me.'

Politically, they are on the same side, liberal Democrats. Jack had supported the ill-fated campaign of Edmund Muskie to be elected in 1972, and had previously helped Senator Eugene McCarthy, but hadn't been seen on many political platforms.

There was, of course, a similar closeness with Walter Matthau. In 1974 they were ready for their joint stage début in *Juno and the Paycock*. It was at the Mark Taper Forum, part of the Los Angeles Music Center. The play was set in a Dublin tenement in 1922, the year the 'two Irelands' were established and which in 1974, when the bombings in Belfast and Londonderry were front-page news in the American papers, had a distinct current affairs ring about it.

Matthau was 'Captain' Jack Doyle, Maureen Stapleton his wife Juno, and Jack his friend Joxer Daly, who only wishes he could find a useful job and curses the legs that give him shooting pains every time he is offered work. It may not have been quite the way Sean O'Casey had seen it, but with George Seaton taking temporary leave of a Hollywood set to direct, it had plenty to commend it – although the *Los Angeles Times* was not so sure. 'The fear in this corner', wrote Dan Sullivan, the paper's theatre critic, 'was that Jack Lemmon, Walter Matthau and Maureen Stapleton would make a vulgar Hollywood star-trip out of *Juno and the Paycock*. In fact, the production at the Taper sees them so determined to do right by Sean O'Casey that the effect is just a bit inhibited. Wednesday night's press opening was a lovely display of acting craft but not, as *Juno* should be, an experience to take home with you. . . . These two frauds are great fun. Matthau makes Boyle a man who is taking his ease behind a front of permanent gloom, as though anyone who had seen such horrors could be expected to attend to the banalities of daily life . . . Lemmon, in contrast, is all lightness – or seems to be. This is the evening's most satisfying characterization, simply because there are several layers to it.'

Now that sounded complimentary enough. But the earlier comments from the critic's 'corner' stung. It wasn't a scathing attack on two well-loved stars, but Felicia thought it was – and so did Carol Matthau. The two wives were so angry about what they considered to be a slur on their husbands' acting skills and sensitivities that they wrote a letter to Mr Sullivan's editor, which was published a month later.

They said they thought that Sullivan's review was 'obscure and uneducated . . . as empty and arid and sterile as his other criticism. He writes loftily and flossily as though to make up for the fact that he has the opinions of a peanut. His thin and fragile writing gifts compounded by a serious lack of content will never do justice to the grandeur that could occur at the Music Center.'

Now that was hard-hitting stuff. But there was worse to come. Sullivan's statement was 'vulgar', they thought. 'If we may fall into the trap of Mr Sullivan's cheap thinking for a minute, we will point out that the three actors mentioned were not discovered wearing sweaters in Schwab's drugstore.' And they finished: 'We hope you will print this letter despite our love affairs with Messrs Matthau and Lemmon.'

Although Mr Sullivan couldn't quite understand what had upset them so, 'since I was congratulating the husbands under discussion for NOT making a Hollywood star trip out of *Juno*,' he didn't know what to make of their strictures. Only one thing was sure. 'It made my wife furious.'

To some people, attacking Jack Lemmon in any way, on stage, on screen or – worse – as a human being, is rather like pulling a chair out from underneath your own mother. Charlie Murphy for one thinks that. Charlie is an actor. He lives in Hollywood, but he hasn't achieved stardom, he has not become one of those names on everybody's tongue. He can't write his own contracts. But he can tell you that working with Jack Lemmon is an experience to cherish. In *Juno and the Paycock* at the Taper, he played a sewing machine salesman who is also an IRA gunman. Offstage, he became one of Jack's friends.

It was during the play's run that Murphy's father died in Philadelphia. Jack got to hear about it and 'sort of adopted' him. 'I was in awe of him at first,' Murphy told me. 'But we just connected. I think he knew what I felt because of his own father's death.'

Jack helped him with his performance. 'I had an entrance in the first act and asked him if he wanted to buy a sewing machine. He told me straight away that he thought I was putting too much into it. He came into my dressing-room and said, "Murphy, ask that question again."'

Then he took the young man on to the stage and went through that small and seemingly unimportant role again and again until Lemmon thought he had got it right. It was a gesture of help, the kind that Jack thought was the entitlement of every performer on the threshold of his career. 'Jack was standing in the wings, and after I finished, he gave me exit applause. "Murphy," he said, "you took a minute and made it a moment."'

That was not merely praise, it was a tribute from a source more valuable than all the critics outside the theatre. From then on, after every live performance, Murphy got his exit applause. He admits, 'It was mainly from Jack.'

Because Lemmon and Matthau were stars in a town of stars, they had a regular flow of distinguished visitors to their dressing-rooms. Jack always deflected his guests upstairs to the tiny dressing-room of Charlie Murphy. One night it was Gene Kelly, the next Gregory Peck. When there was someone particularly important, he would knock on Charlie's door with the message, 'Hey, Murphy, I've got a biggie for you tonight.'

Offstage, he would take the young actor to ball games, watching the Rams destroy the Cowboys from Dallas. Charlie also joined in Jack's musical diversions. 'Walter sang, Jack played and Maureen Stapleton led the group,' he said. They called themselves Juno and the Paycockers. 'Not many stars care about young players just starting out,' Murphy told me, 'but Jack did.'

Encouraging young people in the industry is a little-known side of Jack's life, but an essential feature of it. For instance, a student sent Jack a script for a twenty-minute film that he had written and asked whether he could give him any advice on it. Much to the student's amazement, Jack not only rang him back but also agreed to take part in the film. The fledgling director thought a friend was having him on, until after four more calls he was invited to make his way to the Jalem Productions offices in El Camino Drive and was warmly welcomed by the star. The student had never made a film before, and there was no question of Jack getting any money for the part; he was just happy to help someone get his foot on the ladder.

'I'm beginning to feel like the old man on the set,' he said, aged fifty. 'Sometimes I get kind of resentful. These younger people somehow have a great knowledge of film. I don't know where they get it. Probably from the film departments of universities, and they're deadly serious about it.'

He is one of the most approachable and accessible stars in Hollywood, and when it came to getting a film celebrity to present the awards for the student section of the Academy, it was obvious that Jack would be asked – and that he would accept.

One thing was sure about Jack Lemmon, he was getting older and looking older. If he were determined to avoid doing the things that had become a trademark in his earlier years, it didn't mean that he was not going to experiment. He didn't need the money.

Experience had shown for him, as it had not shown for others, that he was allowed to make mistakes without suffering undue consequences. Jack had decided that the time had come to be brave.

Perhaps the bravest thing of all was to decide to give up drinking. But it didn't last. In 1976 he was given a thirty-day suspended jail sentence with a fine of $315 for driving under the influence of drink. A Highway Patrol vehicle heading north on the Coastal Highway thought Jack's Rolls-Royce was being driven too slowly and ordered the driver to stop. That was when he saw it was Jack Lemmon at the wheel. At the sheriff's sub-station, Lemmon was questioned and breathalized. He was 'booked for investigation', and Felicia received the call she would rather have not had. He was released in her custody. Whether she emptied another glass of water over his head when they got home isn't clear. What is certain is that she wasn't at all happy about it.

It disturbed Jack considerably, too. He had been guest of honour at a stag party and had been plied with drinks. There was a show and later he had some more wine. But he had not had anything to eat. By the time he was ready to go home, he was feeling distinctly woozy. But he drove just the same – because Felicia was at their Malibu beach house and couldn't come to collect him. The unfortunate thing was that Jack knew he was slightly intoxicated and that was why he was driving slowly. It was two o'clock in the morning. At the police station, Jack 'flunked' the intoxication tests – 'by *that* much' as he later reported, indicating that it wasn't much at all. This didn't fit in at all with the various Lemmon crusades on behalf of the ecology movement – pollution by anyone's definition, and he was upset.

Jack was put on probation for two years. It rankled with him, because being a citizen to him meant behaving like a citizen. That was why, when he saw a traffic snarl-up near his home at Tower Road, he got out of his own car and played traffic cop, standing in the middle of the road and directing the vehicles into safe lanes. On another occasion he was so fed up with speeding kids in their cars and motorcycles in his select area of Beverly Hills that he stopped one of them and made a citizen's arrest.

Smoking went the way of his drinking. He still enjoys wine, but he has given up most of the really hard stuff. In the same way, the three or four packets of cigarettes he used to smoke a day were dispensed with. He would wake up coughing in the middle of the night and then light up because he was awake. One night he decided to give it up. When he woke up, he threw the packet across the room and replaced it, not with the cigars which were his usual substitute, but with a pipe. He lights and puffs it from time to time, more, he says, a nervous habit than anything else.

He was perfectly aware of the changes in himself. In 1973 he had told *Show* magazine that the earlier Lemmon had been 'outrageous' and 'selfish'. As he said: 'I wasn't really capable of thinking about anything else. I was so bloody consumed with myself, with acting and music, that I really wasn't aware of what was going on around me. I had no social conscience whatsoever. I really was just blind to everything but acting.'

But after more than twenty years in the business even he knew he deserved the praise. He took part in a Lemmon retrospective at the San Francisco Film Festival. 'I just love these question-and-answer sessions,' he said after seeing a succession of extracts from his movies. 'I've never seen so many of my clips at one session,' he added, sounding a bit like a little boy. But none of this self-congratulation was going to be allowed to get in the way of sheer hard work. 'The business of an actor is acting,' he would tell interviewers at the drop of a notebook, and nothing was going to be allowed to get in the way of that fact. 'Security is all very well, but if one is an actor, it's the parts that are important.'

For most of the time it was a sensible way of thinking and equally sensibly acted upon. *The Prisoner of Second Avenue* looked a little like Harry Stoner with a sense of humour and was nowhere near as good. But it certainly wasn't one of the weaker Lemmon offerings and had him co-starring with one of the sexiest women in Hollywood, Anne Bancroft. If it was the *Tiger* man making people laugh, it was also Neil Simon appearing to dramatize his latest session with his shrink. Jack was an unemployed clerk – with a sexy (and employed) wife – suffering the problems of living in a big city. But given the opportunity of joining up with the men behind his earlier film, he would have set fire to his own apartment and not merely a dress factory. Some critics gave the impression that they would have appreciated that fate for the movie, but it would have been unfair – and would have deprived audiences of an enjoyable if not so memorable evening out.

He was conscious more than ever of the problem of being sure that people did react to his performances. At the time he made *Prisoner* he said: 'Unlike a painter or a writer an actor can do nothing without an audience. If you stand in front of a mirror acting out Shakespeare, you are wasting your time. For me, acting is an intellectual process of divining something. Finding out why a character says what he says, does what he does. Once you've gone through that delicious hell of investigation, the final step is the performance.'

It was not a lasting impression and didn't linger on for *Alex and the Gypsy*, which began life as *Love and Other Crimes*. Then it was called *Main Man and the Gypsy*. Changing a title doesn't usually work as a talisman for changing a picture's luck. It is all too often a signal that something is wrong, and this picture was very wrong indeed.

The biggest mistake was allowing Jack Lemmon to make this picture, which was neither funny nor a good example of his acting. In fact, people watching the movie might have felt entitled to ask for the credits to be run again halfway through the picture. Was this boring nonsense really headed by Jack Lemmon? Fortunately for him, he was operating under such a layer of make-up that one could be forgiven for not being sure – and kindly souls wouldn't have pressed the point.

Jack played a bail bondsman chasing Genevieve Bujold, not simply because it was always a good idea to chase Miss Bujold but because she had run away both from him and from her bail obligations. Miss Bujold looked lovely as a gypsy. Jack apparently looked better showing his 'tushy' (described by one critic as resembling a wrinkled prune) in *Avanti*.

It was, critics pointed out, the one occasion when *all* the people sitting in a Lemmon audience were expected to dislike the character he played – like it or not, there was a great deal about Harry Stoner with which an audience could identify. In

Alex, absolutely nothing. Even Courtney hated it – or, rather, she hated the character he played. Alex wore a thick moustache and Courtney said that it tickled every time she kissed her father. If he didn't shave it off, ten-year-old Courtney was going to elope. He would have done better to accept her ultimatum than continue to make the film, which was about as close to a disaster as he had yet come in his thirty-seven-picture career.

Courtney and he saw eye to eye on most things. There were none of the problems he had experienced with Chris, although on that front things were looking better, too. At the age of twenty he had come down from the moon, or that other mysterious planet where Jack feared his son had taken up residence, and started talking to him.

It started with an unexpected visit. He just walked in the door and said to Jack, 'Hey there, here I am. How are you?' And everything was great again. Chris was taking an arts course and that pleased his father, too. Their holidays together became easier events to deal with. They took a log cabin in the ice and snow of Alaska – and risked colliding with the local bear population. 'The thing to do when that happens is to scream and yell at the top of your voice. That frightens the bear off. Believe me, you don't have to be told to scream. I hollered so much I couldn't speak for a week,' Jack said. Another time he broke a leg when he fell into a hole in the midst of a carefully orchestrated operation fishing for trout.

He did somewhat better in *The Entertainer* on ABC television. It was a role originally played by one of the Lemmon idols, Laurence Olivier, a man whom Jack respects more than anyone else in the acting profession. The part, in the play written by one-time angry young man John Osborne, was straight out of the English music hall. Olivier played him in an ill-fitting tweed suit, bowler hat and more ham than is readily available in a pork butcher's shop. Lemmon followed the Olivier example, with local variations. Instead of the story being set in a British seaside pier show at the time of Suez, Archie Rice, Lemmon style, was an old vaudevillian down to his last cigar stub working in an entertainment park at Santa Cruz, California, in 1944. And instead of the bowler, Jack was given a soft felt hat to match his soft tweed suit and constitution.

The ABC production wasn't universally approved. The *New York Times* said: 'Jack Lemmon plays for schmaltz the role that Laurence Olivier created as a symbol.' But the paper did also say that he 'captures the deadness in Archie's eyes while moving frantically with the automatic gestures of a ventriloquist's aging dummy'.

It was good both as a Lemmon role and as a Lemmon performance. Jack thought so, too – and this time it wasn't being said just because of the commercial advantages of doing so. The play had been booked well in advance by advertisers. 'You can smell that awful old theatre,' he said. 'Literally smell it. It's the kind of quality that I, as an actor, can appreciate and every actor who ever lived will understand – that terrible, terrible lonely feeling of being up there on stage, playing to a handful of people in an eight-hundred-seat house and knowing that you're bombing out, that it's not going over, but that you have to keep on. It's the loneliest feeling in the world and it's there on film.'

And that was what was different about Jack Lemmon. Not once in his career had he ever had to face that sort of audience – certainly the people at the Old Knick were a lot more appreciative. But he could understand what it must feel like to be in that sort of position. What really bugged him was the suggestion that it was all so easy, doing the kind of acting for which he was famous. He told Douglas Keay of the *Guardian*, 'Some people think I'm just funny. They come up to me and say, "You're so natural. Thank God, you don't act." I feel like hitting them on the mouth, because I've knocked myself out trying to be natural. Sure, there are certain innate personality traits in any actor which are almost impossible to cover up entirely. But as far as I am concerned, I haven't the slightest idea what those traits are.'

That was why, like many another star, he wriggled uncomfortably when he saw impersonations of himself – generally regarded as the supreme compliment and the sincerest form of flattery. There was only one man who did that regularly on American television. And as Jack revealed, he didn't feel happy about it at all. 'All the while he's doing impersonations of Jimmy Stewart and such like I'm laughing. But when it gets around to doing me, I just sit there staring. Is that me? Do I go on like that? I don't believe it. Yet the audience is in hysterics and when I look round at my own family, they are also hysterical, looking at me looking at this fellow on the television in total disbelief. I must say I admire the guy. If I had to do a typical Jack Lemmon thing I'd have no idea where to begin.'

Other stars, equally flattered about being impersonated, might find a lot of rude things to say about the impersonator.

Jack leaves the insults to Felicia. One evening they were watching television at home. It was a political programme and Jack thought the main speaker made a lot of sensible suggestions for curing the world's great problems.

'That's what they said about Hitler,' said Felicia.

Jack wouldn't agree. 'Just listen,' he said. Felicia didn't listen. She took up where she had left off the night of that Cagney dinner. She threw a glass of wine in his face.

This time, Jack was able to reply. He yelled a series of epithets at her and chased her through the house and into the arms of their Spanish cook, Rosita.

That had to be the end of the row. He looked at the amazed woman – although she must have heard similar demonstrations of affection before – and said : 'Ugh, me actor. Me rehearse. Me do lines. Me work!' With Jack Lemmon as your boss, you just had to believe it. He was, after all, the man who signed his letters 'A. S.' – 'America's Sweetheart'.

At that, all Felicia could do was to mumble under her breath something like, 'Me love that son of a bitch' and dissolve into his arms, laughing her head off.

Ask him, and Jack would probably say that Felicia was his principal guard against getting caught up in the star thing, his main bridge connecting him with reality. Others were his business interests. He was part-owner of one of Beverly Hills' smartest restaurants, the Bistro, and this helped finance his art collection. Everyone welcomed Jack Lemmon as a customer. He could be seen at some of the smartest night-clubs in town. When a place was 'in', like Dominick's, it was often because Jack was a patron.

Another passion was his golf. Jack was playing the game now with real dedication, and whenever there was a golf junket of the sort to which the stars gravitate, Jack would be there smiling for the cameras and glaring at the ball – for he still wasn't all that good. As Richard Quine told me: 'He would love to be a great golfer. But he has the guts of a lion and plays in every tournament, every pro-am that exists. He gets real stage-fright when the cameras are on him and always makes the worst shot of his lifetime.' But he doesn't play because it is the thing to do. 'He adores it,' says Quine. Jack also always wears some of the best golf clothes seen in the game – usually lemon-coloured outfits.

His own club is the Hillcrest, which is almost totally Jewish. 'I'm the token goy,' he jokes. The club was set up as a reaction against the others in the area which declared themselves 're-stricted' – in other words, they wouldn't allow Jews further than the lobby. (The Los Angeles Country Club went a stage further, refusing to admit people in show business at all.) Hill-crest is not only mostly Jewish, it is almost entirely show business. It is the place where Al Jolson used to hold court to contemporaries like Eddie Cantor, Jack Benny, Groucho Marx and George Burns. 'I'm the only one left at the table now,' Burns told me in 1983, 'but there are compensations. I see Jack Lemmon there.'

The actors at the club are comparatively few. But there *are* directors, producers, agents and accountants, the people who keep the business in show business. To qualify for membership, people have to be regarded as good citizens – and to have given a fortune to charity (the amount is audited before membership is accorded). Jack qualified on both counts.

Walter Scharf, composer of film musicals and musical director of a score of movies from *Holiday Inn* to *Hans Christian Andersen*, occasionally bumps into Jack on the golf course. 'He is,' Scharf told me 'as everyone knows, one of the nicest men in Hollywood. But being with him on the golf course is not a pleasant experience. Other people go to play golf to have a good time and thoroughly enjoy themselves. Jack Lemmon playing golf is like a woman having a baby. Every shot he takes is so long-winded that you end up hating him because he takes it so seriously.'

Melville Shavelson, when we talked about Jack, had no doubt that he was taking his golf *too* seriously. 'It is not good for him to spend as much time on the golf course as he does; he is not as good a player as he is an actor and golf doesn't provide him with the recreation it does to others. He treats it like work.'

Jack would probably dispute that view. But one man who plays with him frequently is a very strong golfer indeed, the actor Steve Forrest. 'His golf is not as bad as Laurence Welk's,' he told me. 'Welk can make every shot seem like the Phoney War. Jack says he is a scratch golfer, so you shoot the course at par, and of course, he does better than that. He is not a scratch golfer! But he is endearing. I've seen him struggling through the rain and the fog and the wind and the cold – sleet, hail. If you haven't seen him doing that, then you've missed one of the great delights of this world.'

Jack had suffered that, year in year out, at the annual Bing Crosby tournament at Carmel, California. He never misses it, always arranges his schedule to be there. The cameras never miss him either. They concentrate on the champions – and then turn to Jack Lemmon 'stabbing' the ball. As Steve Forrest said, 'It could go any way – as it could with any of us, of course.'

Hollywood agent and artists' manager George 'Bullets' Durgan describes Lemmon as 'like a little Teddy bear'. Once he met Jack at a Palm Springs golf tournament. 'I got the feeling, as he sat drinking, that he was feeling lonely,' said Durgan. 'I went up to him and asked if he wanted to go out. We went to a place called Pal Joey's – there was an ulterior motive, I had an act opening that night – and he was just marvellous. We had a good table and sat there while people came up to him, gave autographs, people took pictures with him. He was talking to everybody. He is just a very warm guy. That's a dear man.'

When he wasn't playing golf Jack was looking for something new to do. After his film *Airport '77*, released in 1977, he really had to think about that. Why he made that film after the *Gypsy* shocker is a mystery to most of the people for whom Jack Lemmon still spelt quality. 'It's my first comic-strip part,' he said at the time. There was no evidence that he needed the money to make this third in the series of *Airport* movies, all of them disaster films in the sense that something terrible happens to the plane at the centre of the story. Admirers of Jack Lemmon were disappointed to see him wearing the same kind of uniform Dean Martin had worn piloting the aircraft in the first *Airport* film. They thought Jack was above this story of a private plane crashing with a load of passengers and art treasures – even if it did have James Stewart playing the millionaire who chartered the aircraft. In fact, he put the same effort into *Airport '77* as he had into *Save the Tiger*. For what it was, he did the job exceedingly well and with the usual Lemmon quality.

Jack doubtless regarded it all as a means of subsidizing some of the less lucrative things he did for the ecology movement – like *Plutonium: Element of Risk*. There was an element of risk in striking out into yet another aspect of his war against pollution, but it turned out to be another milestone in his career.

The film, again directed by Richard Quine, was shot partly on Lake Arrowhead and partly at Jack's own home in Tower Road in Beverly Hills. It became one of a series of five documentaries about the environment – covering water and air pollution, pesticides and nuclear waste, the last film written by Jack's friend Don Widener, who had been responsible for the earlier environmental programme and had himself written a study of Lemmon. There had been a certain reluctance to allow Jack to narrate the series – the TV moguls thought it ought to be done by an authoritative journalist. The Public Broadcasting Service rejected the show on these grounds and also because they said there was no spokesman for the nuclear industry on the programme – even though they had sponsored it all to the tune of $124,000. The show was later seen, just the same.

The programme explained the dangers of the substance produced when uranium is burned, revealed the apparent lack of care in its handling, and talked about how dangerous it was both to health and world peace simply by being stored in various parts of the United States. A single accident could put out of action the multi-million-dollar power plants being built in America at that time, leaving cities and rural communities without electricity and with a high risk of contracting cancer. Narrating this shocking indictment of the risks taken ostensibly on behalf of progress, Jack was getting involved in a subject that would before long absorb him entirely.

9
Tribute

If Jack was the sort of actor who put a great deal of himself into his work – and he always has been – then it has to be assumed that a play about a man who can't relate to his young son and who himself has marital problems had to be right up his street. Particularly if he had an opportunity to play the piano and talk a great deal about the theatre. Apart from *Juno and the Paycock*, which played only on his home turf of Los Angeles, *Tribute* would be his first major theatrical appearance since *Face of a Hero*, and as successful as that play had been a monumental flop.

The first two factors didn't really ring true any more in the summer of 1978. Chris had now become an actor, too. He was finding it difficult to get the right parts, but with a father like Jack there was no chance of his starving in a garret, and Dad was helping him find the odd job of work – although emphasizing that, even if he could open a few doors, it was up to Chris himself to keep them ajar. He also had learnt a lesson from his father. There was no better way to relax than to play the piano.

As for Felicia, their unarmed combat continued unabated to the continued fascination of everyone who knew them. Jack himself had put it fairly succinctly: 'There is a lot of "I-hate-you" between us, or "I-can't-stand-you-any-more, I'm-leaving". But never, "I-don't-love-you".' In fact, he would often tell people, 'With Felicia I discovered I could let all my aggressions hang out, which was something I could never do with another human being.'

He felt the necessity to 'hang out' those aggressions because he was still finding himself in trouble – like the one fairly ordinary morning when he discovered his attempt at restraining the family dog, Virgil, could have involved him in a boundary dispute (the cement blocks laid down to hold the fence they were building turned out to be on his neighbour's property); spilled a cup of coffee all over his new trousers; found Felicia had driven away with all the documents he needed to give to his car insurance adjuster; and went to the Beverly Hills Hotel for an important meeting when he should have gone to the Beverly Wilshire.

Jack fitted the role of Scottie Templeton, the theatrical public relations man who made every activity into a party and himself its life and soul. Only one incident in the play, fortunately, did not ring true. Scottie Templeton was dying of leukaemia, still joking, still making conversation that sounded like Neil Simon dialogue – the play was by Bernard Slade, who had written the highly successful *Same Time, Next Year* – and still playing the piano. It was that mixture of comedy and tragedy which made it so ideal for the Jack Lemmon of the late 1970s.

The story was based on that of a real Hollywood agent called Harvey Orkin, who could solve problems that would drive ordinary citizens in search of the nearest psychiatrist's couch – like the time when one of his star clients failed to turn up for a TV chat show; Orkin went on instead.

Every incident in the play had happened to Orkin – or to a friend of his named Jerry Davis – and knowing that helped Jack enormously, for even the most outlandish situation had the tinge of reality about it. The only pity was that Slade wasn't able to use the story Jack thought the funniest of all. Orkin had been unable to find a taxi as he stood on the corner of Fifth Avenue and 64th Street in New York. He was standing with a beautiful woman who was carrying a Pekinese. The weather was dreadful, the streets were awash with the rain that was bucketing down.

They tried to get on a bus, but the driver wouldn't let them on. He said that no dogs were allowed on buses. Orkin, who had solutions to problems before anyone knew they were problems, somehow or other acquired a pair of dark glasses and a white cane. When the next bus came along, he pushed his companion on to the platform, took the dog in his arm, and tapped his stick as he got on the bus himself.

'Just a minute,' said the driver, 'I thought all seeing-eye dogs were German shepherds.'

Harvey thought quickly. 'You mean', he said, 'he isn't?'

It didn't take a guide dog to deduce that *Tribute* was going to be a huge Broadway hit. All the confidence Jack professed to have in his ability to crack this toughest of all theatrical nuts was being put to the test, and after the first night he knew he had a winner.

It was virtually a one-man show, and Jack wrote all the music he played. It was also a show within a show – with people who had had parts in Scottie Templeton's life coming out on one corner of the stage or the other, paying their tribute to this very funny, very human man – and then recalling incidents that would be acted out once the curtain went up. This could have been a dangerous device that fell flat into the orchestra pit, but it worked splendidly when it opened for its try-out runs at the Colonial Theatre, Boston, and the Royal Alexandra at Toronto.

Time magazine's Gerald Clarke said: 'The other actors supply the tears, but most of the sweat comes from Lemmon, who gives his best performance in years. It is comparatively simple to make a character mean or nasty, lovable or funny. Capturing charm, that most elusive of all qualities, is much harder. Dropping all the irritating mannerisms that have marred his recent movies, Lemmon makes the task seem like ease itself. He is a better actor than he usually allows himself to be and if it does nothing else, *Tribute* has restored him to the profession.'

What the magazine said about the play and Jack's performance in it was tribute enough – except that it ignored much of what Jack had done in a profession that was his before Judy Holliday changed that tyre, and which he had never left. What about *Save the Tiger*? Mr Clarke must have been suffering from amnesia. Certainly, it was true he had never done anything better on a stage, and in this performance he was proving himself to be better than most of the other Broadway stars.

It was as much a financial hit as a critical success. The entire $270,000 investment was repaid by the management on the first night – at a party at the Tavern on the Green restaurant off Central Park. Very few plays had earned back all the money invested by opening night, and the producers had never before paid back the money that evening. In fact, it had earned an operating profit of $277,000 on the try-outs alone, which meant a dividend of $7,000 to be shared out among the investing 'angels' before it actually reached Broadway. What had really made *Tribute* a blue-chip investment was the fact that the screen rights had already been sold for a million dollars and Morton Gottlieb, the producer, had taken delivery of a down payment of $300,000 from Paramount.

After a string of wonderful reviews from all the leading New York newspapers everyone knew that Jack would be dancing on that seventh cloud. He himself was only afraid that Felicia would take the opportunity to deplete his bank balance at the sign of a good notice. 'Take her to Brooklyn, and drop her at the nearest army surplus store,' he instructed his chauffeur. 'But keep her away from Fifth Avenue.'

At the party at which the good news of the play's success was revealed, Jack was fêted like a prince. Lauren Bacall was there. So were the inevitable members of the Lemmon set, Walter and Carol Matthau and Jean Stapleton. Once more Jack was denying that Scottie Templeton was a part that had a lot of himself in it. 'There's nothing in him that I can relate to. He's weak, never faced any responsibility. Like a lot of people, he won't make a commitment to try, even if it means failure.' Felicia joked that she knew who Jack was thinking of when he went on stage – Walter. 'Otherwise, he couldn't do it.'

It was obviously a time for tributes. Variety Club International paid one to him on American television. He didn't enjoy the experience – until it was all over. Everything was geared to make it the kind of tribute they thought Jack would like, with special emphasis on his music. His compositions were given the full treatment, while Jack himself looked more sheepish than he ever had on the big screen. They were sung by Paul Anka, whose 'My Way' had made a multi-millionaire a multi-multi millionaire, and Leslie Uggams. One of Jack's *Tribute* compositions was given new lyrics by Alan Jay Lerner, and Sammy Cahn wrote words to another Lemmon tune. All Jack's leading ladies were there. Christopher played the piano.

It was a pleasant show, but Jack gave the impression he would have preferred having his toenails pulled out. 'Oh, God,' he recalled soon afterwards. 'It was so embarrassing. I'd rather open in *Hamlet* with no rehearsal. I guess in everyday life, when someone pays you a compliment, you usually blush, but imagine being complimented for a whole hour on national television. You feel you have to do something in return – like dropping dead, or at the least retiring.' Fortunately nobody wanted him to do either – and he didn't.

The black-tie gathering for the show raised $240,000 for the Thailians Community Mental Health Centre at Cedars-Sinai Hospital. Henry Fonda, Lucille Ball, Edie Adams, June Allyson, Debbie Reynolds and Tony Curtis took part in what was described as 'the greatest turnout in the history of Hollywood'. It was said that it was a justified tribute to a man who 'had to be an actor because the only other thing he could do was play the piano in a whorehouse'.

James Stewart spoke in praise of an actor who is 'beloved by everybody in the picture business and he's a decent human being –and that's why we're here'. Shirley MacLaine told him, 'We're here to honour you for your sweet self as well as for your extraordinary talent.' And from Billy Wilder there was the expected comment: 'He's a consummate actor who can do a short schtick like nobody since Chaplin or Keaton. He's also a citizen, a terrific piano-player – and a lousy golfer.'

To that Jack answered: 'No actor has ever had more important, more wonderful parts, more marvellous directors and writers and more wonderful fellow actors to work with. But of greatest importance has been all the friendships and the relationships and the love I've been able to establish over the years with the people I've been lucky enough to meet and to work with.'

Now he had another film to make. But first, perhaps as a gesture of gratitude for all the luck he had had, he took part in the 1978 National Bible Week as one of a group of actors involved in a Bible-reading marathon. Jack read extracts from the Old Testament. The reading team answered one question: it takes ninety hours to read the whole Good Book aloud.

The China Syndrome, which put the flesh of a story and the visual Lemmon presence on the message of his earlier plutonium documentary, was to be a movie in the *Save the Tiger* class – but a harder task to carry off, for this time he had the formidable competition of Jane Fonda.

It was an intense, worrying, frightened Jack Lemmon, as different from the red cabbage-spilling, lovable guy as had been Harry Stoner the garment manufacturer. Yet now he was no corrupt businessman trying to keep the right side of bankruptcy. He was a much simpler guy who suddenly comes to the conclusion that he has a potential nuclear disaster sitting in his lap. He played Jack Cladell, the manager of the operations room in a nuclear power plant in California, who realizes that the slight tremor felt one morning was, in fact, the harbinger of a radio-active calamity. It all happens under the gaze of a television crew, the cameraman Michael Douglas – who was also the film's producer – and reporter Jane Fonda.

The power station is Lemmon's pride and joy, but Douglas and Fonda see the agony in his eyes and before long know the whole story – fought against the backdrop of sceptical opposition from their own television company and increasingly violent obstruction from the owners of the power station. It all ends desperately unhappily – with the Lemmon character vindicated only in his death. Once again, he put his own stamp on a performance to the extent that audiences wriggled uncomfortably in their seats, almost frightened beyond their own imaginations of what radio-active calamity was awaiting them as they left the theatre.

That, of course, was precisely what Jack hoped would happen. Long before making *Plutonium: Element of Risk* he had worried about the risks of nuclear contamination. Now it unnerved him. He hoped that people who wouldn't stay the pace in a dry television documentary would go to a theatre to be entertained and remain to consider and then worry.

What he could not possibly have known at the time was that, soon after the film was released, a situation even worse than the one shown in the picture would actually occur. For the moment, however, when he signed the contract and when he stood on the studio floor or in one of the various location sites, it was a job he had to do, an opportunity to demonstrate his skill.

He had by this time accepted what others had been saying for years – that the anxiety came across from the screen in his eyes, without a single word necessarily having to come from his lips. In this film, the agony was more than evident – it shouted, it pleaded. It was more than just a dramatic *tour de force*. It was a virtual necessity, since so much of the dialogue involved complicated scientific verbosity which Jack, no more than did most of his audience, couldn't hope to understand. And that produced much of the pathos, too – like the time near the end of the movie when in a room he had himself sealed off from the rest of the power station's staff, he was given an opportunity to explain his case to television audiences. Instead of galvanizing them to the disaster on their doorsteps, he bamboozled them and himself with the jargon. He was to describe jostling with this problem as his biggest single challenge. It was an opportunity to lay his talent on the table, just as the theme of the film opened his heart.

The China Syndrome of the title referred to the fact that the core of the reactor could melt downwards into the earth so that, figuratively speaking, it would reach China at the other end of the world. It would also, of course, spread radio-activity for miles and miles and make most of that part of California uninhabitable.

The film was sold by Columbia Pictures in a way that had never been used before – spending $3 million on television commercials which were described by a Columbia executive as the 'first tease-by-TV' campaign in history. But before long there would be an almost unnatural need to calm down the publicity that quite unwittingly was being thrust upon them.

The stars of the film did not turn up on screen until the second commercial. They were not named until the fourth. It was also part of the psychology in selecting the movie's title. Originally it was going to be called *Eye-witness*, then *Power*. But, explained Jack Brodsky, a Columbia vice-president, they were too easy, too obvious. 'The minute someone says, "What does the title mean?" they're halfway to buying a ticket.' The advertising slogan used said it all: 'Today only a handful of people know what it means –

and they're scared.' The first commercial showed a fiery ball over which a voice of doom declared: 'The China Syndrome. It's not about China. It's about choices. Between honesty and ambition, career and conscience, responsibility and profit.' In addition, a series of promotional video tapes were made and offered to local television stations – which was really revolutionary in March 1979 when the film was first released. Jack got himself involved in it all. He saw the producers of the video in his office at El Camino and discussed every foot of tape with them.

The film opened to the kind of reviews that his previous incarnation in Save the Tiger would like to have heard. Vincent Canby in the New York Times said that Jack Lemmon gave his best performance in years, which considering what he had been doing so recently in Tribute was quite something. It confirmed what Jack had been saying for so long – that the trouble with success in stardom was repeating his former standard. Schoolboys getting top marks and excellent reports could understand what he meant – it is a lot easier improving from the bottom than maintaining a position at the top. 'The China Syndrome,' Canby wrote, is good and clever enough to work on several levels simultaneously – (1) as a first-rate melodrama (will the big bomb be defused before it's too late?); (2) as a satire of big business, including the television news industry in which the people who present the news become more important than the news itself and (3) as an ageless morality play about greed and vanity.'

The New York Times questioned people in the nuclear power industry all over America after attending previews of the picture with them. Could these problems – principally of 'melt down', in which part of the radio-active core would escape – happen as a result of a comparatively minor mishap? The people they interviewed thought that a minor incident could trigger much more serious problems, but they squabbled among themselves over the possibility of even a minor incident occurring.

At the beginning of March 1979 it was merely a theoretical exercise that none of them had contemplated. At the end of that month it became a vivid reality that they had to face much more seriously than the mere hypothesis offered by a convincing film and a brilliant actor.

At Three Mile Island, south of Harrisburg, Pennsylvania, early in the morning, workers on what was affectionately called the 'lobster shift' were startled to see lights flashing and dials behaving erratically. At first – as in *The China Syndrome* – it all was put down to a small fault, like a warning light coming on on a car's dashboard simply because the bulb connection was faulty. Before long they knew better. Days later, highly contaminating radio-active steam was seeping from the plant, and pregnant women were evacuated from the vicinity. One telling line in the film had proclaimed that an accident such as the one occurring in the script 'could render an area the size of Pennsylvania uninhabitable'.

Time, after saying, 'Lemmon, through the sheer integrity of his playing – no cute stuff, no obvious plays for sympathy – is outstanding', had noted: 'A member of the audience might have trouble applying justified scepticism to *The China Syndrome*'s central premise when everything else about the film runs so fast, rings so true.' An accompanying article decided that nothing in the world, from a bicycle to a steel mill, was totally safe and conceded that, yes, there could be a melt-down of the core and a deadly cloud of radio-active gases could be released – in theory. It also said that experience had shown that nuclear power stations' safety devices worked. Two weeks later, the magazine was reporting the catastrophe at Three Mile Island.

He was in his car, driving to a lunch in honour of veteran director George Cukor, who had directed him in *It Should Happen to You*, when he heard about the accident. When he discovered what had happened, 'I damn near went off the road.' Unlike Harry Stoner in *Tiger*, Jack Lemmon always had his car radio tuned to an all-news station.

At the lunch he was swamped by reporters asking for his view on what had happened, as though the man who operated the switches in the film had suddenly become a real-life expert on the hazards of nuclear power. It was at that moment he decided not to attempt to cash in on what might have seemed a gift from a plutonium-polluted heaven. The studio and Michael Douglas told him they had taken a similar decision. It immediately cancelled an appointment that afternoon to take part in a local television station's discussion on the dangers of nuclear power, and an appearance later that day on the *Tonight* show. Jane Fonda had no such compunction, although her motives were not to publicize the movie so much as to take a political stand. With the support of her husband, Tom Hayden, she sent off a personal letter to President Jimmy Carter, demanding that he sack James R. Schlesinger Jnr, his Energy Secretary.

As for Jack, no matter what was said he would appear to be cashing in on the disaster. For more than a week the newsmen hounded him, and for more than a week Lemmon avoided them. Normally one of the most accessible men in the Hollywood community, he wouldn't answer a telephone call that had not been previously vetted. It was too soon to make any comment, though Jack could see that the aim of the film – to awaken people to the fact that these accidents can and will occur – had been achieved in a more emphatic way than he and the others at Columbia had ever envisaged.

Like it or not, the incident at Three Mile Island – much, much worse than the one forecast in the film – *was* having a dramatic effect on the box office. So much so that the New York stock exchange was telling a very encouraging – and to Jack, highly embarrassing – story. In two days, shares in Columbia soared from $22.1 to $24.75 – while the value of nuclear plant stocks declined by an even greater amount. Naturally, none of that hurt Jack. Instead of taking a salary, he worked on the basis of commission – ten per cent of its *gross* rentals, which meant that nobody could deduct all the hundreds of deductible factors involved, like publicity costs. It was worth a staggering $4 million to him within a couple of months of its world première.

Columbia said it was the biggest 'non-holiday' film in the company's history. It was also, without doubt, Jack's most successful movie to date – and only a very short time after telling reporters that there was no chance in the Hollywood of the 1970s of making the sort of money he had learnt to expect at the beginning of the 1960s.

The change of title for the film paid off more handsomely than the television commercials – which were promptly stopped. Quite suddenly, a new phrase had entered the vocabulary of the nation. 'We are not in a China Syndrome situation,' said a spokesman for the power station company, without appreciating the irony of it all.

The year 1979 was Lemmon's silver jubilee in Hollywood. Twenty-five years undoubtedly led to introspection – of just the kind he was not yet ready to have with *The China Syndrome*. The most evident effect of the anniversary was to contemplate yet again the seemingly strange relationship with Felicia. 'She's my rock,' he told British writer David Lewin. 'Without Felicia, I don't know where I'd be. We need one another and together we are complete. We can't function without one another.' As he noted, there were not many families in California who could say that. As far as his career was concerned, he was not beyond thinking about failure – but he tried not to worry about it. 'The important thing to realize is that failure doesn't hurt anyone – in fact, you learn from it.' Some might say that only someone as abundantly gifted with success could afford to say that. But he explained: 'The fear of failure can stop people doing things and they go on right down the same old road all their lives. They don't go down the alleys and they don't try. And then, when you get run over by a truck or a producer and end in the gutter just the same, you say, "Why in hell didn't I at least try? How bad can the view from the gutter be – so long as you are looking up?"'

He was looking up all the time. *The China Syndrome* produced yet another Oscar nomination, although he didn't win this time. But he did get the British Academy award, Italy's David de Donatello prize and the NATO Star of the Year award. At the 1979 Cannes Film Festival he was given the Best Actor title. He was also nominated for a Tony for his stage role in *Tribute*, which gave him considerable pleasure. When he did allow himself to speculate into the future, he still thought he would like to play Hamlet – even if it would have to be an aged prince not conceived by the Bard. He also had dreams of playing Cyrano. 'I would love to do *Waiting for Godot*, too,' he said. 'But most of all, I want to do *Son of Tribute*.' Which was almost exactly what was about to happen.

If he had doubted the wisdom of his next Hollywood decision, the nomination for his Broadway Tony would have convinced him to go ahead. He was now to start earning his share of the contract with Paramount to make the film version of the play – but not before starring in it on stage once more, this time in the Huntington Hartford Theatre in Hollywood. Seeing Lemmon's *Tribute* on stage was one of those experiences that left me wondering how such a remarkable stage actor had ever allowed himself to be directed into any other medium, and why others had consented to his live performances being confined to his own country. Making the film was plainly the next best thing, although I was struck by the fact that Jack Lemmon, whose two faces – comedy and tragedy – were now so evident, was a different performer again in the flesh.

To do the part for the film, he had to look *almost* as sick as Scottie Templeton looked at the end of the movie, wracked with the terminal effects of leukaemia. In one week Jack lost five pounds. He had to discipline himself to lose even more during the following seven days. The methods used to give the same impression on stage would not be acceptable on screen. In the Brooks Atkinson Theatre he had worn suits and shirts specially made two or three sizes too big at the end of the play. His own question-mark posture made him look even leaner – and he bent himself forward to achieve just that. 'Damn near ruined my spine doing it,' he recalled.

It was going to be more exciting, working on the part in front of the cameras, he said. As he said: 'I don't know another actor, including Marlon, who's had as many marvellous roles as me. And my good luck is that they've been spaced over the years.' He knew this was going to be another one. Despite the things said about the play, Jack thoroughly enjoyed playing Scottie Templeton. *Tribute* seemed to be the perfect cocktail of comedy and drama – and a connoisseur of the martini (still insisting no one put an olive in it) appreciated that. He believed he benefited from the Templeton role because it was an opportunity to hide behind a character. He didn't think the wisecracking PR man was like him at all, and he always appreciated the opportunity to play men with whom he couldn't so obviously identify. Those were the most fun to do.

Tribute won him not another Oscar, but at least another nomination certificate (his seventh) to hang on his study wall. The film was not universally praised, although his own performance received most people's approbation. From *Films Illustrated* came the comment: 'It is not that it seems inflated for its subject, rather the opposite – the material is not up to the talent it is supposed to be celebrating. It gives the actor nothing new, merely the opportunity for reprising past routines.' The *International Herald Tribune's* Thomas Quinn Curtiss said: 'Jack Lemmon is a farceur of skill and the role is tailored to his talents. He has exactly the proper style for its delivery, making the most of the Broadway *bons mots*, the insouciance with which the flashy fellow counters embarrassments, and allowing a peek at the concealed distress that motivates his occasional fits of exasperation and dread.' To which one might be forgiven for asking, 'What more is needed?'

One of Jack's complaints was that the film was seen by too many people as a picture about death. He saw it more as a vivid endorsement of the need to live – and enjoy the process. 'It's like *Save the Tiger* in that respect,' he told Charles Champlin in the *Los Angeles Times*. 'A man discovering he's had his priorities bolloxed up.' Then he went on, 'Am I going to have to sit around for another year waiting for something half as good? I have no desire to sit back and take it easy.'

It wasn't going to take anything like that. In 1981 there were two new roles up for grabs. One of them was with his buddy Walter Matthau, appropriately called *Buddy, Buddy*. That was a highly sensible decision, playing with Walter again. Even more sensible was to take Billy Wilder's idea for a story, accept his script and agree to play in anything his old buddy, buddy was directing. What was not so sensible was to say, as he did about practically everything he was about to undertake, that this was the 'very best'. In this case, he was saying it was the very best comedy script he had ever read. It couldn't have been – although it was funny. It was pleasant to discover that at last we were seeing something of the old Jack Lemmon, the one who, given a stretch of street to walk down, would always find the bit with the hidden manhole. In this case, he was the one who fell into a bath full of water – when trying to hang himself in the bathroom – and who was always about to fall from a ledge high up on a building.

Buddy, Buddy, originally to be called *A Pain in the A—*, was about two men in the same hotel in Riverside, California, for distinctly different purposes: Jack to commit suicide after failing to patch up his broken marriage, Walter to assassinate a witness at a grand jury hearing at the courthouse over the road. The trouble was – and there has to be trouble in a Lemmon–Matthau film – that the confounded potential suicide was obstructing the assassin's view. But the kind of things expected of the vintage klutz were conspiring to make Jack less than comfortable. 'I'm a lover, not an athlete,' he complained to Wilder when asked to undertake yet another stunt. Playing his part in sopping wet clothes for the two weeks it took to shoot the bathroom scene was merely a preamble for all that followed.

When the director tied a wire around his middle – to protect him if he fell from the hotel ledge – he quipped: 'I do think that being over fifty I'm a bit too old to be doing the Peter Pan bit for the first time.' He was in fact fifty-six. The truth was that the Peter Pan Lemmon, the one who gave every sign of never knowing how to grow up, was the Lemmon many people liked best. When, in another scene, he was expected to escape down a laundry chute, he said mournfully: 'Even as a kid, slides were never my thing. Matthau pushes me down and I have to scream on the way down. Believe me, it didn't take much acting.'

Matthau did his own share of stunts – and his own falls. When one of these went wrong, Billy Wilder told me, it was an opportunity to witness the unadulterated love the two men have for each other. Walter fell eight to ten feet on to a cement floor, after taking a wrong step. Jack flew off in his direction. 'He raced down the staircase where we were standing and rehearsing the scene. He bent over him – and it was just the most touching thing. They are like brothers. Like father and son – I don't know who would be the father and the son.' It was this that made *Buddy, Buddy* as acceptable as it was – although Wilder said he wasn't sure that they should continue to make so many films together. 'I think they should continue, but not too many together – because they're pretty Goddam good by themselves and they can carry a picture on their own. But it's marvellous to watch them. If anything bad happened to one of them, they would first call each other. Lemmon would call Matthau, not the police or the ambulance, God forbid.'

If there *was* a special spirit between the two men, it showed itself in abundance during the making of *Buddy, Buddy*. As Jack said: 'Working isn't the word. Every day is a party on set with Walter.' One day, there was a special party. It followed a time when even Billy Wilder seemed cantankerous. He wasn't happy with what was going on. He didn't like the way Matthau dragged Jack out of a car. He did it first with his leg. 'Don't do that to me,' cried the director. 'People will think we're idiots.' When Walter changed it to a pull of Jack's shirt, he said: 'We're getting closer to the moment of sexual fulfilment.' Then he said it was okay, 'but I think we can do it better'.

On the fourth take, he said 'Print' and discovered there had been a hair over the lens. So it was shot twice more. When that was done, preparations were made to shoot a second scene in the same garage – except that it was broken up by the entire cast and crew gathering around Jack and singing 'Happy Birthday'. He was then presented with a lemon-coloured cake complete with little lemons made of marzipan. It was because everyone thought Jack's heart was made of marzipan that they so readily joined in the celebrations.

This was his seventh film with Wilder, the fifth playing alongside Walter. 'I take one look at that face of his,' he said. 'It's like the map of the world and I just double up. It's the only time that filming is fun. The rest of the time I worry.'

He worried a great deal about *Missing*, his second movie of 1981. No more was he trying to get laughs from falling into baths or from twisting his face into the kind of grimaces that make women all over the world want to take him in their arms and pat his back. This was serious, more serious than *Save the Tiger* or *The China Syndrome*, but no one knew when that film was being made how close to reality the story really was. It was the first film in which Jack played a man who was living still, and played him under his real name.

Once more, Jack would have been able to make his usual disclaimer – the part of the New York businessman, Ed Horman, was nothing like the real Jack Lemmon. Lemmon was a liberal, who understood other people, who knew how to laugh. Horman was a solid conservative, the kind whom you expected to wear gloves before shaking your hand. Like Lemmon, he had had trouble with his son, whose values were not his at all. Unlike Lemmon, they had not found out how to see eye to eye.

He didn't approve of the way his son lived or where he lived, in Communist Chile. Most important, he didn't approve of the son's wife, played by Sissy Spacek. The picture was directed by the eminent Greek Costa-Gavras, who had directed the acclaimed political film Z.

When his son disappeared in the 1973 Chile revolution – the one that overthrew the Allende government, the world's first and only democratically elected Communist regime – he went in search of the young man. That was what Missing was all about. Jack conveyed the agony Horman felt by magnificent understatement.

Jack denied that he took Missing because of the political connotations. 'They just came to me,' he told friends who congratulated him on the fine political statements he was making in the movies. 'The film-makers just came to me with good ideas.' As always, he took his own ideas to the making of the movie, prepared though he was to accept the director's view as final. In this case, he wasn't aware that the mere exchange of ideas would sometimes be difficult, since Costa-Gavras's English was not as fluent as he had imagined.

Near the end of the picture there was a scene that he found very difficult. It was one of the most emotional parts of the film in which he and Sissy Spacek argue. At the end of the scene, both felt emotionally drained. Sissy had tears in her eyes, a gesture of happiness and satisfaction that the filming for the day was complete – and appreciation of the marvellous performance by her co-star.

She went up to Jack and said, 'Give me a hug.'

The director heard this, and called to an assistant director in his halting English: 'Here, give her a . . . a . . . 'ug.'

Jack doubled up. 'I've been working with this guy all these months and thought he understood what I was saying,' he said – and the whole company virtually collapsed, while an incredulous Costa-Gavras looked on, not knowing why he had caused so much merriment in the midst of the heavy story.

It wasn't just a moving performance by Jack, it was quite

probably the performance of a lifetime of outstanding performances. The only doubt I have heard expressed about it came from Jack's old friend Billy Wilder. '*Missing*,' he told me, 'was a very, very good picture in which he himself was very good. But I thought that he was too serious in that picture. If a comedian gets into one of those serious things, and this was a thrilling picture, he can do too much. It was a performance drenched with heaviness and *too* depressing.'

Needless to say, the picture was not shot in Chile itself. Even asking for permission would have been impossible. The Latin American atmosphere was captured by filming in Mexico. Jack studied the role as he always did, but the one opportunity that would have enabled him to get to know the part best of all he denied himself. He refused to meet Ed Horman himself until after the picture was finished. 'I did not want to meet him,' he told *American Film* magazine. 'Many actors might want to meet him because they might feel they could learn something or get something from the real Ed Horman. If you're going to play MacArthur or Truman, or anybody famous where a great percentage of the audience is going to know that person, you're locked into something. You have to speak a certain way, because he's known. But Ed Horman was not known. If I can treat him as if he was fictional, as most characters are, then I'm not inhibited.'

He didn't even talk about the character very much to Costa-Gavras. They had a good relationship and Jack was able to put much of his interpretation together based on thoughts he had on the plane journey from Los Angeles to Mexico. Gavras would ask him if he wanted to rehearse. Jack said, 'No. Let's roll.' As he explained: 'I got so excited, I couldn't see straight. Like going to the gym if you're an athlete and working out.'

And the excitement showed, even if it were a deep, underplayed excitement. Audiences experienced with Ed Horman the torment of a father searching a pile of bodies for his son. Why did the American government fail to do more in Chile? The question is never answered – other than with the suggestion that Charles Horman was disposed of because he knew too much and that the State Department decided it was politic to look the other way. The patriotic American Republican who believes that the Stars and Stripes and all its agencies are not just fundamentally good but the founts from which all goodness springs is brought face to face with the double standards imposed by Richard Nixon and his policies.

The film brought statements of outrage from the State Department. It issued a three-page document denying the authenticity of the story, the first time they had ever taken action of that kind. Jack said he loved their reaction. It publicized the film and he was delighted that it should. 'I thought it was a dumb thing for them to do. It just brought enormous attention to the film as it was coming out, even before word of mouth would do it.'

They issued no denials when the book on which the film was based, *The Execution of Charles Horman*, was published by his lawyer, Thomas Hauser, possibly because it came and went without selling many copies. Now Jack knew they had a hot potato on their hands, shovelled out of the oven by a Jack Lemmon film. He realized he had got over the message at the first preview. He was sitting in the balcony wondering how a live audience would react. A character on screen talked about the wonderful things in the American way of life. A man stood up in the theatre and shouted: 'Bullshit.' Jack never thought the picture would alter State Department policy, but he was convinced it would make people think about what was happening in their name. 'Not everything the government says is right,' he said. 'And it is not always working for our best interest.'

When the film was released, the clash of real events was almost *The China Syndrome* again. Newspapers carried stories of more seemingly unimportant, uninfluential people vanishing in Chile, a country that the White House was helping to finance now that the Communists had been evicted. When on a chat show Ed Horman was asked if he felt bitterness to the people responsible for his son's death, he said, 'No, just what people can do.' As Jack said: 'It was such a simple and honest statement that I just started to cry.' Suppose that boy had been Chris, he kept thinking.

Jack said he was not interested in scoring political points. But, 'What troubles me is the way we accept and condone the corruption of morals – not by villainous heavies, but decent people who can do indecent things and rationalize them. . . .

We've reached the point that the crime isn't in the act but in getting caught. And if you do get caught, you can make a million dollars. I really hope to encourage people to think about such things.'

The film was taken to the 1982 Cannes Film Festival and Ed Horman went along with Jack for the ride and for the numerous press conferences. It was a worthwhile journey. The picture shared first prize for Best Film (with the Turkish *Yol*) and Jack won the prize for Best Actor. The finest comment came from Horman himself. 'I worship this film,' he said. Real people portrayed by other people on screen don't often say that.

There was another personal connection that Jack had with the *Missing* story. In October 1982 he and David Clennon, the actor playing the duplicitous American envoy in Santiago, helped Mrs Renate Kline investigate the death of her son Michael in El Salvador. They helped pay the cost of bringing the body back to Los Angeles for an autopsy.

Jack's politics did not spoil his relationship with Ronald Reagan. Before *Missing* was released he and Felicia had received an invitation to the White House. President and Mrs Reagan were gracious, he said afterwards, despite the attack the film makes on a Republican government policy. But as Jack said: 'Ronnie was blameless in this.' The Lemmons went to Pennsylvania Avenue with press agent Jim Mahoney. The President took them to his gym and, still wearing his presidential suit, demonstrated that he was a dab hand with the equipment. He then confided that he had already seen the picture – the American Film Institute had provided him with their only existing print. 'Jack gave a splendid performance,' said Reagan.

That certainly was the reaction of the critics. The *New York Times'* Vincent Canby wrote: 'If *Missing* were only an inventory of the details of Charles's life and disappearance, it wouldn't have the terrific emotional impact that it has. Mr Lemmon and Miss Spacek are superb and their increasing respect and fondness for each other as the story unfolds gives *Missing* an agonizing reality.'

Once more Jack was nominated for an Oscar – only to be pipped at the post on this, his eighth nomination, by Ben Kingsley for his portrayal of the title role in *Gandhi*, a movie that swept all the boards at the 1983 ceremonies. But Jack was gratified by the support from people who might not have shared his political beliefs. When the MCA-Universal boss Lew Wasserman hosted a lunch at Cannes for Jack and the other people there from *Missing*, he paid tribute to the fact that not once were political considerations raised by the studio when considering whether or not to make the picture.

Jack also had the satisfaction of knowing that the film was admired both by the critics and the public, which had accorded him a status reserved for very few figures in the motion picture world. All over America, Lemmon retrospectives were being organized, following the showing of three of his films at the Museum of Modern Art.

Practically everyone was saying the same thing. One thing that was not missing was Jack's talent.

10

The Great Race

Of all the things said about Jack Lemmon while researching this book, it was his golfing friend and sometime acting colleague Steve Forrest who summed him up: 'He has real convictions. He really cares.' He probably wouldn't have achieved as much if he didn't.

Other actors have seen things happen in their lives and put them into their films. Other actors have related to situations and because they have done so have made better jobs of their performances. What Jack Lemmon has done has been to use his skills as an actor, his devotion to his craft, as a means of making himself that much more of a man. He has a full range of emotions and has used them all on film. He knows that sad men sometimes laugh and clowns cry. That is why the Jack Lemmon of the 1980s isn't the juvenile in trouble of the 1950s, or the young executive who always gets the coffee in his lap and the door in his face of the 1960s. His is constantly evolving. Shakespeare knew about the ages of man. Jack demonstrates the fact every time he appears on screen, playing his own age – so that his films are a marvellous record of how *this* man has changed, even though experts in the art of the cinema, such as Frank Capra, still say that his greatest potential is still to come.

'I look back on my movies making the rounds for the 500th time on TV and I'm beginning to look like my own son on the screen,' Jack says. 'I don't think everything was better in the old days. I like the young directors coming out of college.'

Because he sees himself as an actor before everything else, he knows that his task in life is to act. That is why he rarely appears to slacken off. Certainly he doesn't slacken as a human being. Soon after completing *Missing*, he heard that his young protégé Charlie Murphy was in hospital. The actor who had charmed, and been charmed by, Jack in *Juno and the Paycock* had been in a serious road accident. Jack heard about it just before Murphy was about to be discharged. The patient was sitting in the doctor's office when Jack arrived there.

'If you'd answer your Goddam phone, Murphy,' he said, 'you'd know I'd been ringing you. I'll take you home.'

Murphy said he had a friend who had agreed to do that for him, but suggested an alternative. 'If you want to go to the Tail of the Cock,' said the younger man referring to a well-known hostelry on Los Angeles' Sunset Strip, 'I'll be there.'

He did just that. At the Tail of the Cock Lemmon bought the drinks – and dishes of clams and oysters, too. Then he phoned Felicia to say he would be late home.

Murphy was grateful. It was a marvellous display of Lemmon friendship after two months in a hospital ward, but he was embarrassed at all this attention – and money – being lavished on him. The innate sensibility of the actor spotted this. 'Murphy,' said Jack, 'do you have a dime in your pocket?'

'Yes,' said Charlie.

'Well then, will you lend it to me?' He knew it would make Murphy feel better to see that he was contributing, somehow, if only in this token form, to the bill. He told him: 'You must have had a great time in the hospital, getting laid by all those beautiful nurses.'

Murphy replied: 'All the prettiest nurses had blonde moustaches.' They both laughed. 'It was like being with an old friend,' Murphy told me. Which was another part of the Lemmon persona.

He demonstrated it again soon afterwards on an overseas trip with Walter Matthau. With their wives they went to Israel on an exploration mission organized by the United Jewish Appeal. Several other well-heeled and well-known men were on the trip, including Arthur Hiller, who had directed Jack in *The Out-of-*

Towners. It was Jack's first visit to the country and he came back telling all who would listen how impressed he was by everything he saw. It was a two-way experience. Walter and he were received by the then Prime Minister, Menachem Begin, and met other important people in the country. But these were not the ones who made the biggest impression – or those who were most struck by Jack Lemmon.

They went to a children's hospital where Jack suddenly became a combination of favourite uncle and Santa Claus, if that isn't a contradiction in Israeli terms. 'These were all crippled children and some of them were retarded,' Hiller remembered. 'It was very moving for all of us, but Jack sort of sat in and played with the children – and how much fun they got out of it! It was lovely to see how well known Jack and Walter were when they got there. What I liked about it was how they would both enter into conversation with people and indeed initiate conversation.' Hiller already knew that Lemmon was the kind of man you *could* talk to; now he saw it in action.

As the United States 1984 election season got under way, in the early months of 1983, Jack was immediately sought by the Democrats to be one of the hosts of its fund-raising 'telethon' in which millions of dollars were pledged by viewers of a twenty-four-hour TV spectacular. For this programme – one of his very few political statements in public – he took as his theme his favourite hobby horse, the environment. The Democrats were the party that he believed would do most for the ecology movement. When people asked why he didn't do more, he replied: 'I haven't used my clout as an actor to influence people because I'm not that politically astute.' Others would recognize that as being fairly typical Lemmon modesty. He understood the message of his films, and no actor had been so politically influential for years.

If he had said it with that Lemmon chuckle in his voice, people would have understood just how serious he was. In 1983, when his beach house at Malibu was swept up in the fires that ravaged California and was severely damaged, he went on to keep a previous engagement, talking with his usual good humour to the students at ULCA, the University of Califoria at Los Angeles.

Approaching sixty, Jack still had ambitions – to direct a comedy film and to do a play in London were just a couple of them. He wanted to do more plays on Broadway, too, but, as he said, the problem was never knowing if the show would last for a year or a night – and he had the worry of taking Courtney out of school at a critical time in life (in 1984, she was seventeen). One thing was sure, he had no plans to retire – 'until I'm run over by a truck. Or, possibly, a critic.'

As he told the *Los Angeles Times* in 1983: 'I just love it. It's been good to me. I've given everything I can. And I get a tremendous boot out of my work. And I'll just keep right on going.' Shirley MacLaine said she thought he was the only actor who has no conceit. To which Jack replied – worrying, no doubt, that he would sound conceited, 'Well, that's nice of her. I just hope it's true.'

Age was making an impact on him. His close friend, contemporary and former business partner Richard Carter had died of cancer. A few years earlier he had been one of the principal mourners at the funeral of Jack Benny. Now he was saying: 'The older you get, the more the phone rings. And a friend has died. If you can become unaware, or less concerned, well, you're a better man than I am, Gunga Din. You become a realizer. You could catch something tomorrow. You could get hit tomorrow.'

But he had constantly to remind himself that he had done very well. 'Knock wood,' he said in 1981, 'everything's going just fine.' With a career and marriage like his it certainly was. He ages well, and hopes he won't become one of those men in their sixties who slim down, wear shirts open to their navels, have long chains round their necks 'and look like a couple of horses's asses'.

He isn't one of those performers who yearns to be young, although he felt he could have been in better shape when he made *Buddy, Buddy*. As he said at the time: 'Young bones can take this kind of torture, but I was sore for days. Worse yet, I think it affected my golf score over the weekend.'

Above everything, Jack's secret has been to earn the sympathy of his audiences, even in parts like *Save the Tiger* when he should be inciting them to throw things at the screen. I. A. L. Diamond had an explanation for that: 'People are rooting for him to straighten out, because of their tremendous identification with him.'

He succeeds because he always puts so much into it, because he doesn't leave his character behind every time he sheds his clothes at five o'clock, because he works at it to the point of weeping at the wheel of his car, because he knows the character will eventually find him. But why does he do it? He told me: 'If you do know how to do it, either you have done it before or there isn't a hell of a lot to get. But if you do not know how to do it and are a little afraid of it, then that excitement and that little bit of fear make you do your best work. You'll really work at it.' And it's always a new experience for him. 'Actors have to be accepted on a much larger scale than most people – like sports figures. Each time I give a performance I feel I'm coming up to bat all over again. I am riddled with professional insecurities and it gets harder all the time.'

He sees acting as being therapeutic. 'I believe that there are an awful lot of actors who may be emotionally screwed up – but if they weren't actors, they would be so screwed up that they'd be locked away. I think that acting is a tremendously healthy process. Its main appeal is that we'd all *like* to do it. We all do it as children, but as we grow up we are taught that we're not supposed to do it.'

Billy Wilder saw that. I asked him if he thought Jack was happier doing comedy or the tragedies which were playing a much bigger part in his working life. 'He just likes acting,' he said. 'You were at school. You know there was always a boy who wanted to get on the stage and then he was happy. Well, that's Jack.' And then he said: 'It has been my experience that most actors can offer you one and perhaps two types of items before emptying their shelves. Mr Lemmon, however, is Macy's, Gimbels and Sears-Roebuck – catalogue and all.'

Melville Shavelson just wishes he didn't spend so much time on the golf course. 'You have to get him between golf games to speak to him these days,' he told me.

Since Jack did like analyzing things, he was quick to pinpoint the actors whom he admired most: Alec Guinness, Ralph Richardson and, of course, Laurence Olivier. He later added Marlon Brando to that list. 'All of them have a magnetism that is as important as their talent,' he said as long ago as 1956. He means it still. He even used to applaud when Olivier came on television for a Polaroid commercial. That is true appreciation. Now there are other actors who would put Jack Lemmon at the top of the list.

He is the first to admit that he enjoys the trappings of success, although he no more flaunts them now than he would have done in earlier days. His Jaguar and his Rolls-Royce are not status symbols. He doesn't need them – but he does like them. Never will he make the outrageous demands to producers that other stars insist upon. His greatest pleasure still comes from his piano and pool table that are usually installed alongside the sets before he moves into a film studio. Off the set, he'll still say that, apart from being on the golf course, he is happiest fishing. But he is full of nervous energy, and can seldom truly relax.

What people like about him is that when they meet, he still greets them with a grin and a warm handshake, and will apologize for the stain on his trousers caused by the cup of coffee he has just spilt. You still get the feeling that any minute he is going to walk into a closed door. They say he is Mr Average or Mr Everyman, and he is not ashamed of displaying characteristics of average men who, on average, like to keep those things quiet. Only there's nothing average about the way that he does it. He told British broadcaster and writer Barry Norman: 'True success is achieving as much as you can within your own limits.'

The incredible thing about Jack Lemmon is that he doesn't really apear to have any limits.

Some actors, he once said, only come to life when they are playing somebody else. 'That way they can lose their guilt. I haven't lost all my guilt. But I sure don't need to be somebody else.'

If he did, he wouldn't be the man his audiences like so much. Nor would he be the man to knock wood, looking at his family, his home and the eighty films that have earned him those awards. Above all, *we* wouldn't be able to walk into a theatre playing a Lemmon movie and quote his opening line on the studio floor: 'Magic time. Ter-rif-ic!'

Index